1985

Evaluating Teaching Effectiveness

Evaluating Teaching Effectiveness

A Practical Guide

Larry A. Braskamp
Dale C. Brandenburg
John C. Ory

With the Assistance of

Eileen Kohen
Paul W. Mayberry

SAGE PUBLICATIONS, INC.
Beverly Hills / London / New Delhi

For information address:

SAGE Publications, Inc.
275 South Beverly Drive
Beverly Hills, California 90212

SAGE Publications India Pvt. Ltd.  SAGE Publications Ltd
C-236 Defence Colony   28 Banner Street
New Delhi 110 024, India   London EC1Y 8QE, England

Printed in the United States of America

Library of Congress Cataloging in Publication Data

Braskamp, Larry A.
   Evaluating teaching effectiveness.

   1. College teachers—Rating of—United States.
2. College teaching—United States—Evaluation.
I. Brandenburg, Dale C. II. Ory, John C. III. Title.
LB2333.B7   1984   378'.125   84-9942
ISBN 0-8039-2341-4
ISBN 0-8039-2342-2 (pbk.)

FIRST PRINTING

CONTENTS

PREFACE AND ACKNOWLEDGMENTS

This book is first and foremost a practical guide intended to assist faculty and administrators critique, design, and implement evaluation of teaching on their campuses.

Although this guidebook is practical in its intent and contents, we have written it from the point of view that the evaluation of teaching should be assessed from a variety of perspectives; that is, no single piece of evidence (e.g., ratings) collected from one source (e.g., students) is sufficient to judge the competence of a teacher. When put into practice, this principle becomes a multiple purpose, criteria, source method approach in this guidebook. A second major principle in evaluating teaching effectiveness is that the purpose of the evaluation, such as personnel decision and improvement, needs to be taken into account when evaluating. Purpose is related to use in our thinking; that is, the use to be made of an evaluation needs to be determined before an evaluation is undertaken.

We consider our approach to evaluation to be within the current mainstream of thinking of faculty evaluation, at least the thinking of our colleagues who write and conduct research in this area. The current consensus is that evaluation is a complex, dynamic undertaking and that sole reliance on student ratings, the most common strategy in evaluation to date, is not sufficient. We also regard our approach to be consistent with the position on evaluation of teaching taken by the American Association of University Professors as noted in the report of Committee C on College and University Teaching, Research, and Publications (1975).

The numerous origins of our thinking about evaluation as presented in this book are based both on our experiences as evaluators in our office (Measurement and Research Division, Office of Instructional Resources at the University of Illinois, Urbana—Champaign) and the writings, ideas, conversations, and debates with many colleagues over the past decade or more. Although we can't mention everyone, we want to acknowledge some of our colleagues and briefly state how they have influenced our thinking. Robert Brown (University of Nebraska—Lincoln) helped form our view of evaluation as being fundamentally a human enterprise in which communication between the parties is a key part of the evaluation process; Barbara Gross Davis (University of California—Berkeley), has demonstrated a thoroughness and informal style of working with her clients worth copying; Ernest House (University of Illinois) helped persuade us that since evaluation is not infallible, we should regard it as a form of argument and treat it as a guide to action. Donald Hoyt (Kansas State University) has greatly helped promote the important role of credibility in evaluation by viewing it as a political and perceptual issue apart from the technical problems of validity and reliability; Martin Maehr (University of Illinois) has helped us see the need to place evaluation within the context of a person's motivational pattern; and Wilbert McKeachie (University of Michigan) has presented three conditions that are necessary for faculty to change their teaching behaviors based on feedback about their teaching, one being that alternative ways of behaving must be presented before a person can change. This idea has influenced us on the role of feedback in facilitating improvement. Barak Rosenshine (University of Illinois) assisted in our conceptualization of a hierarchy of student rating item types, especially the differentiation of high and low inference items. Michael Scriven (University of Western Australia) has distinguished assessing the worth versus the merit of a faculty member, and this distinction is embedded in our thinking on the uses of information. Richard Smock's (University of Illinois) emphasis on the symbiotic relationship between evaluation and development has made us more aware that these two activities are not totally independent of each other. Robert Stake (University of Illinois), who has tirelessly argued an evaluation should incorporate different value-perspectives, has not only influenced our thinking but many in the field of evaluation.

Many of our colleagues who hold similar positions at other institutions have also played an important part in our work as evaluators. Ken Doyle and John Centra also provided important leadership in the American Educational Research Association Special Interest Group, Instructional Evaluation, a group that has conducted the lion's share of the empirical research summarized in this guidebook.

In addition, a few of our colleagues played a specific part in developing this book. Many of the ideas have been field tested in workshops at the University of Illinois and elsewhere, including one at SUNY at Potsdam under the leadership of C.R. McKinstry and two at the University of Virginia under the leadership of Sam Kellams. Sam's critique of an earlier draft helped us in our ideas on defining good teaching as a prerequisite to the evaluation of teaching. We also received invaluable feedback on earlier versions of this book from our former staff colleague, David Frisbie (University of Iowa) and from Barbara Gross Davis (University of California—Berkeley).

Materials from many others have been included in this book. The following have kindly given us permission to reproduce their materials: Educational Testing Service; Center for Faculty Evaluation and Development, Kansas State University; University of Virginia; University of Southern California; Augustana College, Rock Island, Illinois; and the departments of business administration and horticulture, University of Illinois, Urbana—Champaign.

Finally, we are grateful to Charles McIntyre, Director of the Office of Instructional Resources at the University of Illinois for allowing us the time to write a guide for the University of Illinois, Urbana—Champaign campus use and for encouraging us to write this guidebook for use on other campuses. We also express our appreciation to Janet Osterbur and Debra Drake, who willingly typed yet another revision.

HOW TO USE THIS GUIDEBOOK

In using this guidebook you should keep the following in mind:

(1) We have broadly defined teaching, and it thus encompasses components such as classroom activities, organizing a course, developing a curriculum, and advising students.

(2) We have emphasized the distinction between two major purposes of evaluating faculty—personnel decision and teaching improvement.[1] These purposes are to be viewed as complementary. Conflicts that emerge from evaluating faculty simultaneously for both purposes need to be recognized and dealt with, but if an evaluation is properly designed and implemented, both purposes can be served with a minimal amount of conflict and with increased efficiency and effectiveness.

(3) "What is the use?" is a fundamental question to ask in any evaluation program of faculty competence. In our view of evaluation, the uses to be made of an evaluation is one of our two overriding principles of faculty evaluation.

(4) The second key principle in our view of evaluation is multiple perspectives. In this guidebook we have labeled it a "multiple purpose, criteria, source method approach." The net result of this view is a very comprehensive approach to evaluation, which, however, can seldom be fully implemented on any one campus. Thus we recommend that you adopt this approach as a conceptual framework (i.e., a way of thinking about evaluation) to help you organize your ideas and plans. Then, as you begin to implement this multiple-perspective approach, your "realism" should emerge and be an important factor in deciding what you can do given your local conditions.

(5) The human side of evaluation is crucial. Evaluation of persons is a deeply personal and sensitive undertaking. We have yet to work with someone who has not been anxious, interested, or

concerned about an assessment of his or her work. But giving advice and suggestions about this side of evaluation is difficult, and thus our concern about the human element in evaluation may not come across as strongly in this guidebook as we wish it to be.

This guidebook is organized into five chapters, with evaluation for personnel decisions and improvement highlighted in Chapters 2 through 5. Chapter 4, the chapter on ways of collecting information about teaching, is organized around the five common sources of information—students, colleagues, self, alumni, and records. For each source we have included a discussion of the technical quality of the evaluative information that can be collected from each source, examples of techniques and instruments, and a list of suggestions for using information from these sources for both personnel decision making and improvement. For a quick overview of the ways that various components of instruction can be evaluated, please read Table 4.1. Table 4.2 lists where in the book the various ways are discussed.

This guidebook was written for three major audiences: (1) departmental and college administrators who have the responsibility of evaluating faculty for annual salary increases and for promotion and tenure, (2) departmental advisory and executive committees, and (3) faculty who desire to collect more and better information about their competence both for personnel decisions and for improving their own teaching.

If you are a college or departmental administrator or member of a committee with the responsibility for evaluating teaching for salary adjustments and/or promotion and tenure, Chapters 1, 3, and 5 and the sections in Chapters 2 and 4 that are headed "Suggestions for Personnel Decision" are the most relevant. If you wish to learn of possible ways to evaluate teaching for improvement, sections in chapters 1 through 4 headed "Suggestions for Improvement" are the most relevant.

If your institution (e.g., system, campus, college, department) has specific policies and practices already in force, you will need to take them into account in using this guidebook. From our experience the best plans are those that are developed locally.

Note

1. Some have equated evaluation for personnel decisions to summative evaluation and evaluation for improvement to formative evaluation.

CHAPTER 1

DEFINING GOOD TEACHING

What is good teaching? How can we define meritous teaching? Can we measure excellence in teaching? Questions of this type have been asked for centuries and they now embody a key issue in the minds of our politicians and civic leaders as the debate on merit pay for teachers escalates.

Unfortunately, there is no set of easy answers to these questions. Research on teaching effectiveness is voluminous and approached from a number of theoretical perspectives. (See Peterson & Walberg, 1980, for a summary of the trends in this research.) The research on effective teaching at the collegiate level has primarily been in two areas. One focus has been on discovering what teacher characteristics are associated with good teaching. The net result of this line of inquiry has been a list of teacher characteristics (closely aligned with attributes, traits, and personality factors) that are used to define the ideal, model, best effective teacher. Although it is impossible to capture the findings in a phrase, the one that comes as close as any in our opinion is the phrase, "hardness of the head and softness of the heart," which Goldsmid, Gruber, and Wilson (1977) used to summarize how students and faculty colleagues define excellence in teaching. (For more information on this topic, see reviews of research by Aubrecht, 1979, 1981; Costin, Grenough, & Menges, 1971; Dowell & Neal, 1982; Feldman, 1976a,b, 1977, 1978, 1979, 1983; Kulik & McKeachie, 1975; Levinson-Rose & Menges, 1981; and McKeachie, 1979; books by Centra, 1980; Doyle, 1983; and Seldin, 1980; and the chapter by Scriven in the *Handbook of Teacher Evaluation* edited by Millman, 1980.)

The second line of inquiry has focused on the relative effectiveness of the lecture method and alternative modes of instruction. Kulik and Kulik (1980) in their review of the research in this area concluded that teaching by the lecture and discussion method are equally effective if the criterion is learning of factual information. However, teaching by discussion is more effective than lecturing if the criteria are problem-solving abilities, interesting subject matter, attitudes, and curiosity. In their review of research on the individualized approaches to teaching such as the Personalized System of Instruction (PSI), they concluded that the personalized instruction modes generally resulted in higher end-of-course achievement, better long-range retention, but not longer student time spent on courses when compared to the traditional lecture method.

Based on our review of the research on teaching at the collegiate level, we think that the research reflects a diversity of conclusions as much as a consensus. Thus no one definition of excellence in teaching is advocated as the standard against which all teaching is to be compared.[1] As a practical guide to evaluating teaching, we think that a good strategy for defining excellence in teaching initially is to consider three major areas that can be emphasized in defining teaching. They are *input, process,* and *product.* Figure 1.1 displays these three areas with some prominent factors in each area. In general, the evaluation of instruction can be divided by its emphasis on input (What do students and teachers bring to the classroom?), process (What do teachers and students do in a course?), or product (What do students learn or accomplish in the course?). A closer look at each emphasis

Input
- Student characteristics (e.g., class level, major field)
- Teacher characteristics (e.g., rank, sex, academic discipline)
- Course characteristics (e.g., size)

Process
- Classroom atmosphere
- Teacher behaviors
- Student learning activities
- Course organization
- Evaluation procedures

Product
- End-of-course learning, attidue change, skills acquisition
- Long-term learning, attitude change, skills acquisition

FIGURE 1.1   Three Major Emphases for Defining Good Teaching

should reveal that effective teaching is defined differently depending on the emphasis placed on input, process, or product.

Input. If input is emphasized, the basis of judging excellence is much of what has occurred before the course even begins; for example, class size, educational backgrounds, and experiences of both the students and the instructor. Often the teacher has little control over these factors and the focus is not on how the instructor behaves in the classroom. Although input factors need to be taken into account (e.g., a large introductory course in calculus), since they may and can influence student ratings and learning, information focusing on these factors will yield a rather incomplete portrayal or assessment of teacher performance.

Process. If process is emphasized, the focus is on what the instructor does both in the classroom and in organizing and managing the course. The questions relevant to process include: What does the instructor require of the students (e.g., assignments, workload)? How does the instructor teach in the classroom (e.g., lecture, discuss)? and, How does the instructor relate to the students both in and out of the classroom? The basis for judging effective instruction centers around teacher rather than student behaviors. However, the linkage between what an instructor does and amount learned by students is not always clear, and thus sole reliance on process factors is also not recommended.

Product. If product is emphasized, the basis for judging effective teaching is amount of student learning. Although this definition has great appeal, there are two major problems in linking student learning to conclusions about effective teaching. First, the measurement of student performance must be done in such a manner that confidence can be given to test results. Do the tests adequately tap what students learn in a course? Second, student ability, motivation, and prior knowledge influence what students learn in a class. These and other factors need to be taken into account in judging the effectiveness of an instructor, and thus student learning is also not recommended as the sole basis for judging teaching competence.

Despite the problems inherent in defining good teaching, certain generalizations about teaching can be made:

- Teaching is related to student learning and deals with establishing conditions for facilitating learning. Thus, evaluating teaching is best accomplished by including the areas of input, process, and product.

- No single instructional strategy is always superior to any other. For example, faculty who lecture are not necessarily better teachers than faculty members who use discussion techniques.

- Good teaching means more than entertaining in front of the class.

- Instructors have different skills, abilities, and preferences, and they should be aware of them and be encouraged to use them.

Note

1. For a prescriptive definition of good teaching, see Scriven (1981), who includes an ethical dimension as well as the role of institutional and professional goals and obligations in his definition.

CHAPTER 2

EVALUATING TEACHING—
SOME CONSIDERATIONS

A campus's evaluation program should be developed keeping in mind two of the major purposes for evaluation—to help faculty examine their teaching for improving it and to help those with proper authority make enlightened decisions about a faculty member's promotion, tenure, annual salary adjustments, awards, and selection into special development programs. Thus the purpose of an evaluation influences the type of information collected, the analysis and portrayal of the information, and the dissemination and use to be made of the information in an evaluation program. However, the development of a systematic evaluation program on any college campus does not guarantee its usefulness regardless of its intended purpose(s). In this chapter we present several considerations that are relevant to establishing a formal evaluation program. These considerations are listed separately for personnel decisions and for improvement.

Personnel Decisions

(1) An inherent paradox in evaluation cannot be avoided. A paradox centers on an individual's quest for excellence (Glass, 1975), a quest that is central in the life of many

FIGURE 2.1   A Needed Linkage If Evaluation Is to Be Functional

faculty members. On the one hand, faculty interested in improving their instruction should specify goals and receive feedback about their progress toward achieving these goals. On the other hand, faculty value and need freedom to explore and to fail, while not continuously being judged by others. Both approaches in striving for excellence are valid, but in conflict. While faculty have an obligation to demonstrate their accountability to those who support them, they also need autonomy and freedom (George & Braskamp, 1978). The major question to ask is: How can evaluation be designed so that the institution can fulfill its accountability to its constituencies and still allow faculty sufficient autonomy and freedom to experiment and to "profess?"

(2) The linkage between performance, the evaluation of performance, and reward for quality of performance is necessary for an evaluation program to have any utility. If no contingencies exist among performance (what the teacher does), evaluation (judging value of what the teacher does), and rewards (rewarding the faculty member in some way for teaching effectively as determined in the evaluation), then evaluation loses its potential and becomes an unnecessary expense in time and effort. However the linkage between the three is strongest when the connections are flexible, fluid, and dynamic. The broken lines between the three activities as drawn in Figure 2.1 are meant to depict this linkage. As March (1980) and McKeachie (1982) have argued, maximum clarity of standards and expectations does not necessarily lead to optimal clarity of standards. If we apply this to evaluation, does it mean that faculty need to know exactly

what they are to do and specifically how their work is to be measured? We think not. In designing an evaluation program, it should not be so explicit that faculty feel the need to behave in certain ways in order to look good in an evaluation. If so, evaluations may be usurping a general working principle of academe—faculty are basically interested in their work and they receive considerable satisfaction from doing their work well. A reward system that replaces reliance on internal motivation with dependence on tangible, external rewards can increase competition among the faculty, which may ultimately reduce rather than increase faculty productivity, especially in the area of teaching (McKeachie, 1982). Therefore a balance between communicating expectations through a formal evaluation program and allowing faculty freedom to rely on their own set of standards is needed. The major question to ask is: Does the evaluation tend to encourage faculty to look good as opposed to being good?

(3) The merit and worth of a faculty member needs to be considered. Merit and worth, as two forms of value, need to be distinguished. Scriven (1978) notes that merit is concerned with the extent to which a faculty member performs work deemed as excellent and of value to the profession or discipline. On the other hand, the worth of the faculty member depends upon the extent to which the person is making a contribution to the local institution. The difference is in institutional dependency, and this difference becomes most apparent when hiring new faculty or considering someone for tenure. For example, a scholar in the foreign languages may be an excellent faculty member in terms of research productivity and teaching, but the local institution with a strong emphasis in technology does not have sufficient numbers of students who wish to enroll in classes taught by this faculty. Consequently, the institution may have difficulty awarding tenure to this faculty member if the institution cannot afford this person on its faculty. This distinction is, of course, a matter of degree, and each institution needs to

decide for itself what the balance can be. As Scriven points out, worth without merit is of dubious value at the very least. Institutions will do well to communicate this distinction to persons at the time of hiring rather than at the time of promotion and tenure when this issue is most acute. The question to ask is: Does the institution make a distinction between merit and worth?

(4) Evaluation is a powerful means by which faculty learn of institutional expectations. When evaluation occurs, policies, values, expectations about goals, workload, and excellence are considered. The determination of criteria, standards, and types of evaluative information to be collected and used is both an administrative and faculty matter and one that is often not without controversy and disagreement. One of the major tasks of any organization in higher education is developing a reward structure in which its faculty can acquire a number of things, such as a sense of worth by doing good work, financial remuneration to do more than exist, and a rewarding place to fulfill their career aspirations. Faculty have a number of personal incentives for working hard and not all faculty have the same motivational profile. External rewards such as salary increases or promotion are not the only ways to reward performance even though they are often more important than is admitted publicly. Recognition is also effective. Knowledge that one is doing good work is a condition for higher internal motivation. (See Braskamp, Fowler, & Ory, 1984, for an exposition on the use of faculty rank to describe and explain how faculty differ in their professional career development. See Braskamp and Maehr, 1983, and Maehr & Braskamp, unpublished, for ways in which personal investment, a primary concept in their theory of adult motivation, is used to describe how motivational patterns influence receptivity to different rewards. For readings on how different organizational theories are employed to describe the influences of institutional policies and practices on faculty behavior and

productivity, see Bess, 1982.) The major question to ask is: Does the evaluation increase or reduce faculty satisfaction, morale, and productivity?

(5) The evaluation procedures need to be incorporated into the departmental and institutional policies for awarding promotion, tenure, and salary adjustments. The measures and types of information used as indicators of instructional effectiveness need to be consistent with institutional policies and communicated to the faculty in advance. The major question to ask is: Do faculty know what information is accepted as legitimate evaluative information?

(6) Evaluation must have credibility to both the faculty and to the administration. Credibility is the perceived trust the participants involved (faculty, administrators, trustees, alumni) can place in the evaluation process and the results of the evaluation. It is a perceptual problem and a political matter. Gaining credibility requires the support of both the administrators and faculty, especially the senior faculty. It is not unlike the practice of participatory management in the business world. For a discussion on the role of administrators in changing teaching evaluation procedures, see O'Connell and Wergin (1982). Furthermore, those implementing the evaluation program must remain impartial and respect the prerogatives of the individual instructor and establish guidelines regarding the confidentiality of evaluations. The major question to ask is: Does the evaluation have sufficient credibility?

(7) Information used in evaluation must be fair. Fairness refers to the extent to which the information adequately represents both the criteria used to evaluate instruction and the complexity of the teaching activities. If the information to be collected does not accurately reflect the activities of the instructor or student learning, the information is incomplete. Thus, capturing uniqueness in an impartial manner is the aim. The major question to ask is this: Does the information

used in evaluation adequately represent the teaching efforts and accomplishments of each faculty member?

(8) Information used in an evaluaton must be of sufficient technical quality. Technical quality refers to the extent to which the information is comprehensive, reliable, and valid. At a minimum, the administrative procedures, the instruments, and methods used in the data collection need to be consistent for all faculty. Student, course, and instructor characteristics (e.g., class size, type of course, elective/ required status) also often need to be taken into account when the information is interpreted for assessing teaching competence. The major question to ask is: Is the information accurate, trustworthy, and properly used for the purpose for which it was intended?

(9) Evaluation must be based on acceptable legal principles and practices in personnel appraisal. An evaluation needs to be based on faculty members' fulfillment of their responsibilities in teaching and on justifiable methods of data analysis and interpretation. Due process in an evaluation is also essential. In general, the courts have not dictated the contents (i.e., selection of criteria or standards of quality) but have focused on procedural due process (i.e., how the evaluation was carried out and how well the institution followed its written set of policies and procedures). Providing legal advice for the general case can be dangerous, so we are brief in this consideration. A number of sources are available that explicate the legal issues involved in performance appraisal. (See chapters 2 and 3 of Latham and Wexley, 1981.) Information about legal issues pertinent in evaluating faculty can be found in Bernardin, Beatty, and Jensen, 1980, and in chapters in books by Centra (1980), Doyle (1983), Millman (1981), Seldin (1980), and Smith (1983). A comprehensive treatment is given in the book by Kaplan (1978). The major question to ask is: Does the evaluation process—the specification of criteria, collection and interpretation of the information, and dissemination—follow legal principles?

(10) Levels of review built into the program make the evaluation more comprehensive, fair, and credible. Multiple interpretations of the information are generally superior to a single person's judgment of teaching quality. Furthermore, factual errors are more apt to be detected and corrected if opportunities for review are built into the process. On the positive side, a consensus achieved through multiple reviews helps make the evaluation more credible and fair. The major question to ask is: Can errors and misinterpretation be detected and corrected before a final assessment of worth or merit is determined?

(11) Evaluation is as much a social and human activity as it is a technical undertaking. Evaluation often is sensitive and deeply personal, especially to faculty who are not yet tenured. Thus the manner in which evaluative information is communicated is a key factor in an evaluation. Personal communication of feedback by a departmental administrator in an annual review has been rated as especially effective by faculty because it provides opportunities for a faculty member to respond to an evaluation and to discuss their career (Braskamp, Fowler, & Ory, 1984). The major question to ask is: How are evaluations communicated to the individual faculty member?

(12) Alternative evaluation procedures can be examined for their benefits to the institution. A comprehensive set of procedures, while meeting most of the previous considerations, may not be feasible due to lack of time and financial resources. The major question to ask is this: How realistic is the evaluation; that is, which procedures must be included and which can be altered or eliminated?

Faculty Improvement

(1) Information collected for improvement is collected for the instructor only. Instructors may benefit by sharing

information with a colleague, but instructors should be able to do it at their own discretion. This restriction is necessary so instructors can have the freedom to ask questions about potential problems without reprisal from those responsible for personnel decisions. The major question to ask is: Do faculty have the freedom to collect evaluative information for their private use?

(2) Information can be frequently and informally collected. Since the information is not intended for personnel decisions, any type of evaluative information can be immediately examined to help the instructor in assessing a course. The trustworthiness of the information does, of course, depend on the reliability and validity of the data. The major question to ask is: Are faculty collecting enough information to monitor their progress?

(3) Evaluation tied to self development maximizes its long range utility. Minimally, a faculty member needs to think of evaluative information as a starting point for further analysis and problem solving. Evaluation, professional development, and improvement in instruction are inseparable. The major question to ask is: Does the faculty member accept the principle that self-evaluation of teaching is a necessary condition for change and growth?

(4) Information collected that is highly detailed, diagnostic, and focused on specific teaching behaviors and course characteristics (e.g., tests, text) increases the usefulness of the information. Information about specific teacher behavior and course features that need improvement is very helpful before specific changes can be considered. Specific information does not result from asking students or colleagues such general questions as "Did you like this course?". Instead, written comments to specific questions or responses to highly diagnostic scaled items are needed. The major question to ask is: From the information collected, can the instructor identify specific strengths and weaknesses?

(5) Information shared with another often increases the usefulness of the information. A consultative relationship between an instructor and another faculty member or a staff member responsible for faculty development is beneficial for many reasons. The relationship allows the instructor to work through some of the personal reactions to evaluations, especially the negative ones. The consultative relationship also provides an opportunity to both learn about and explore alternative teaching strategies. To improve, a teacher often needs to know more than they are "fair," "average," or "bad" in their teaching. It is here that McKeachie's (1982) analysis of the maximal use of feedback is particularly cogent. He stated that persons increase their likelihood of changing if they receive information that is informational (new insights, data), if they are motivated to change, and if they receive information about alternative ways to behave. The major question to ask is this: Do faculty who desire to examine and discuss their teaching have opportunities to receive consultative assistance?

CHAPTER 3

AN APPROACH FOR
EVALUATING TEACHING

Evaluation is ultimately a subjective undertaking. Evaluation is more than description; it requires judgments and interpretation. In this guidebook one of our key principles is that teaching effectiveness can best be evaluated if it is assessed from a variety of perspectives. To incorporate this principle a multiple purpose, criteria, source, method approach is advocated. This approach, as displayed in Figure 3.1, serves as the conceptual framework for this book. Each element in this approach is described briefly below.

Multiple purposes. As noted in Chapter 2, evaluation is undertaken for a variety of reasons. Information for evaluating teaching can be provided to

(1) the instructor for his or her improvement as a teacher;
(2) colleagues for any decisions about the future of a faculty member such as promotion, tenure, termination, special salary adjustments, and annual salary increases;
(3) students to guide their course selection; and
(4) colleagues involved in course and curriculum development.

The first two items are the primary uses of instructor evaluation. From our experience, giving information to students for course selection has not worked very well since the

A

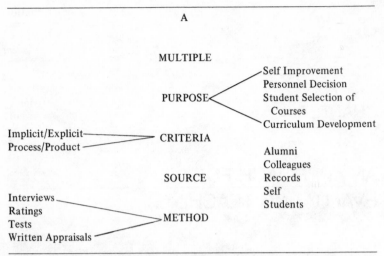

FIGURE 3.1   An Approach to the Evaluation of Instruction

information is often too terse or incomplete, and not all faculty or courses are included in a published list. The fourth purpose of evaluation—curriculum development—focuses primarily on course rather than instructor evaluation. Unfortunately, this function is too seldom employed, especially for courses that are prerequisite or a part of a series of courses in a field of study. Much of the information collected for improvement is appropriate for curriculum evaluation. Instructors who are part of a curriculum committee or team very often can collect information to satisfy these purposes.

The remainder of this guidebook will focus on the first two functions: evaluation as means for instructors to improve their teaching and evaluation to aid in decisions regarding faculty. Table 3.1 presents major features of these two functions. Two features are worth noting: Use affects what information is to be collected and how the information is to be disseminated. If an evaluation's use is for personnel decisions, then information that measures overall competence is preferred. If the use is for improvement, then highly

TABLE 3.1   Major Features of the Two Major Functions of Evaluation

Feature	Evaluation for Personnel Decisions	Evaluation for Improvement
Primary use	Institutional accountability	Personal development
Primary audience	Decision makers	Faculty member
Primary types of information	Judgments of quality Global integrative assessments High inference	Descriptions of behavior Diagnostic, detailed specific Low inference
Primary evaluation strategy	Formal, standardized, legal	Informal, frequent
Primary other person in the evaluation	Administrator of unit	Trusted colleague, consultant
Primary type of information communicated	Judgments of merit and worth to institution	Suggestions for alternative ways

detailed diagnostic information that describes strengths and weaknesses of the instructor is generally preferred.

The purpose of the evaluation also influences the dissemination of the evaluative information. If the purpose of the evaluation is for *personnel decisions,* then those responsible for the decisions—department head, dean, or promotion committee—have access to the data. If the purpose is for *improvement,* then only the instructor and colleagues working with the instructor on a consultative basis have access to the information.

Multiple criteria. Judgments about the merit or worth of an instructor and/or course are based on certain criteria. Criteria are dimensions or characteristics that are used for assessing the effectiveness of instructor and/or course. A number of criteria can be used in judging instructor effectiveness. For example, one is student knowledge of definitions in a specific subject matter. Others are the instructor's ability to communicate effectively, rapport with students, appropriateness of sequence of the course topics, and clarity of the course objectives. In thinking about criteria, it is important to differentiate between the selection of criteria and selection of indicators or measures of a criterion. For example, instructor ability to communicate effectively can be measured by several indicators—student ratings, colleague assessments through observation, and review of lecture notes.

In selecting criteria, it is helpful to distinguish among three types—*input, process,* or *product*—described earlier (see Figure 1.1). Is the focus on the behavior of the instructors or the achievement of the students? The selection of input, process, and/or product criteria should reflect the importance given to each in defining effective instruction. If teaching effectiveness is defined as the amount of progress students make, then student learning and accomplishments are the primary criteria. If teacher behavior is considered the most relevant factor, then the instructor's teaching skills and ability to design a course should be used as criteria. The emphasis on input, process, and product depends on the values of the discipline and an institution's view of teaching effectiveness.

Criteria also vary in the extent to which they are specified, described, and measurable. Explicit criteria, like student test scores and attendance, are directly observable. If these are used, everyone knows the basis for an evaluation. As such they are often regarded as the most logical and rational criteria for assessing value. On the other hand, implicit criteria, such as colleague judgments based on classroom observation, are more qualitative in nature. They are often regarded as subjective because no tangible observable pieces of data are collected. Instead, judgments based on experience are used to assess merit or worth. Both types of criteria are often needed in an evaluation since they complement each other and thus expand the diversity of information collected in an evaluation. If a multiple perspectives approach is adopted, then a variety of criteria are recommended.

Multiple sources. Information about an instructor can be collected from a number of different sources, since not everyone judges an instructor in exactly the same way. Sources include *self, alumni, students, records,* and *colleagues* (which can be other faculty members, departmental administrators, deans, and professional staff responsible for faculty development).

Multiple methods. The final step in the multiple perspectives approach is selecting methods or techniques for collecting the information that best serves as indicators of the selected criteria. A number of ways can be used to collect information about teacher competence and course quality—*achievement tests, ratings and surveys, written appraisals* (comments and critiques in response to open-ended questions), *interviews,* and *observations.* The selection of a method is essentially a measurement task; that is, what procedure or technique should be chosen to obtain the most reliable and valid information?

In sum, the approach outlined in this book emphasizes the importance of multiple perspectives. Information collected from a number of sources and by a variety of methods, each reflecting a diversity of criteria, is the ideal for obtaining a fair and credible assessment of faculty teaching competence. However, in adopting this approach, selections must be made. The next chapter contains some suggestions for collecting information by some of the more common source/method combinations.

CHAPTER 4

COLLECTING EVALUATIVE
INFORMATION ABOUT TEACHING

Any number of combinations of source and method can be employed for collecting evaluative information described in this guidebook. The selected combinations are depicted in Table 4.1. The combinations are mixes of five sources— students, colleagues, self, alumni, and records—and four methods—ratings, written appraisals, achievement tests, and interviews. Not all combinations are equally appropriate to evaluate different components of instructional performance. Table 4.1 is included as a guide in selecting one or more ways to evaluate selected components of instruction given the purpose for which the component is to be evaluated.

In the following pages, the presentation is organized around sources for collecting evaluative information. Coverage of each source includes an introduction to the importance of each source, examples of methods, a brief review of the technical quality of the information collected by a method from a source, and suggestions for using methods or combinations of methods, listed separately for personnel decision making and for improvement. Table 4.2 presents the sections in which these topics are covered in this book.

TABLE 4.1   Components that Can Best Be Evaluated for Improvement and Personnel Decisions by Each Source/Method Combination

Source/Method	Improvement	Personnel
Students		
1. Ratings		
a. Global ratings	B,C	A
b. General ratings	B,C,D,E	B,C,D
c. Specific ratings	B,C,D,E,F	
2. Written appraisals	B,C,D,E,F	
3. Interviews	B,C,D,E,F	
4. Achievement tests	F	F
Colleagues		
1. Ratings	B,D,E	A,D,E
2. Written appraisals	B,D,E,F,G,H	A,D,E,F,G,H
Alumni		
1. Ratings	B,C,F	A,F,H
2. Written appraisals	B,C,F	A,F,H
Self		
1. Ratings	B,C,D	
2.Written appraisals	B,C,D,E,F,G,H	B,C,D,E,F,G,H
Records	D,E,G,H	A,D,H

NOTE: A = Overall Instructor Competence, B = Teaching Skills, C = Relationships with Students, D = Course Structure and Organization, E = Course Materials, F = Student Learning, G = Course Development, H = Advising.

Section I: Students as Sources

Students as sources provide an important and unique perspective, since they are the primary recipients of instruction. Student evaluations can include descriptions, satisfactions, and judgments of value. Students are appropriate sources when they are describing or judging

- student-instructor relationships,
- their views of the instructor's professional and ethical behavior,
- their workload,
- what they have learned in the course,

TABLE 4.2 Sections in Which Scouce/Method Combinations Are Described

Component	Achievement Tests	Students			Colleagues: Ratings/ Written Appraisal	Self: Ratings/ Written Appraisal	Alumni: Ratings Written Appraisal	Records
		Ratings	Written Appraisals	Interview				
A. Overall instructor competence	I.D	I.A	I.B	I.C	II	III	IV	V
B. Teaching skills	–	I.A	I.B	I.C	II	III	IV	–
C. Relationships with students	–	I.A	I.B	I.C	II	III	IV	–
D. Course structure and organization	–	I.A	I.B	I.C	II	III	IV	V
E. Course materials	–	I.A	I.B	I.C	II	III	–	V
F. Student learning	I.D	I.A	I.B	I.C	II	III	IV	–
G. Course development	–	–	–		II.B	III	–	V
H. Advising	–	–	–		II.C	III	IV	V

- fairness of grading, and
- instructor's ability to communicate clearly.

Generally, students are not in a good position to judge the relevance and recency of the course content and knowledge or scholarship of the instructor.

Information from students can be collected in a number of ways. Four common methods are

- rating scales,
- written appraisals,
- interviews, and
- student achievement tests.

A. RATING SCALES

Rating scales include student rating questionnaires or surveys: any type of paper and pencil instrument on which students indicate their responses to items on some numerically based scale. Rating scales are commonly used on most campuses partly because they are the most efficient method for collecting information from students.

In two national surveys conducted in the late 1970s by Centra (1977a) and Seldin (1980), systematic student ratings were one of the most common method/source combinations employed at private and public colleges and at research and comprehensive universities. Over one-half of the private and public colleges used ratings to evaluate teaching, and at universities student ratings as well as chairman and colleague evaluations received the most weight in evaluating faculty teaching effectiveness.

Not all student rating forms are the same. There are three major types, each developed with a different rationale. They are the omnibus form, the goal-based form, and the cafeteria system.

Omnibus form. Items included in this type of form represent major areas of instruction that have been identified through research. The research procedure most often employed, factor analysis, can reveal major dimensions in which questionnaire items can be classified. Results of such studies (Brandenburg, Derry, & Hengstler, 1978; Centra, 1980; Doyle, 1983; McKeachie, 1979) commonly yield the following areas or dimensions of classroom teaching:

- communication skill,
- rapport with students,
- course organization,
- student self-rated accomplishments,
- course difficulty, and
- grading and examinations.

Most omnibus questionnaires include items on these topics. Because the same form is given to all faculty at an institution so that overall comparisons can be made, the name "omnibus form" is used as the label for this type.

The same form is often considered applicable for both personnel and improvement purposes. See Appendixes A, B, and C for the form distributed by Educational Testing Service for use on any campus, and institutional forms developed at the University of Virginia College of Education, and the University of Southern California.

Goal-based form. This type of form emphasizes student learning in the number of areas. Students rate their progress on a number of stated course goals and objectives, such as gaining factual knowledge, developing special skills and competencies, and developing appreciation for subject matter. The IDEA system, developed by Donald P. Hoyt at Kansas State University, is based on this rationale (Hoyt & Cashin, 1977). Appendix D displays the IDEA form. In this system teachers rate the importance of each course objective so that comparison between student ratings of progress and importance on the goals is possible.

Cafeteria system. A cafeteria system is not a single instrument or form. Instead it consists of a pool of items from which instructors have the opportunity to select items they consider most relevant for evaluating their course. The first cafeteria system was developed at Purdue University in the early 1970s and in recent years this method of student ratings has been a common one at Big Ten universities. The Instructor and Course Evaluation System (ICES) used at the University of Illinois at Urbana—Champaign is a cafeteria system (Measurement and Research Division, 1977). The ICES item pool includes three basic item types—*global, general concept,* and *specific*. Items are classified into types by the amount of inference student raters make in answering a given item. Global items require high inference, because students need to make judgments and generalizations from their experience in the course. For example, the item, "Rate the Instructor," requires students to make a considerable amount of inference. Examples of a number of global items are listed in Table 4.3. On the other hand, specific items are essentially descriptive and diagnostic; for example, "Were written assignments returned promptly?" General concept items pertain to areas of instruction, such as those employed in constructing an omnibus form, and require students to make some inference before they answer the item. The ICES general concept and specific items are classified under the following categories: Course Management, Student Outcomes of Instruction, Instructor Characteristics and Style, Instructional Environment, Student Preferences for Instructor Learning Style, and Specific Instructional Settings. (Examples of all three types are listed in Table 4.5.)

The ICES system is designed to take into account two major purposes for student ratings: provide information for personnel decisions and feedback for course improvement. The first purpose is satisfied by the inclusion of three global items (Rate the Course Content, Rate the Instructor, and Rate the Course in General) on every ICES survey form. The second purpose is satisfied by a catalog or pool of over 400 items from which instructors have the opportunity to select items they consider best meet their information needs. Appendix E shows an example of an ICES form that includes the three global items (Numbers 1 through 3) and some general concept items (Numbers 4 through 11) used as a departmental core (common items for evaluating faculty in a

TABLE 4.3   Global Item Examples from Various Student Ratings Questionnaires

University of Illinois

Global Items (6-point scale: Excellent-Very Poor)
1. Rate the Course Content
2. Rate the Instructor
3. Rate the Course in General

University of Michigan

Core Items (5-point scale: Strongly Agree-Strongly Disagree)
1. I would recommend this course to others.
2. I would recommend the instructor for this course to a fellow student.
3. The instructor motivates me to do my best work.
4. I feel that I am performing up to my potential in this course.
5. I had a strong desire to take this course.

University of Southern California

Global Items (5-point scale: Very Good-Very Poor)
1. How does this course compare with other courses you have had at USC?
2. How does this instructor compare with other instructors you have had at USC?

University of Minnesota

Global Items
1. How would you rate this instructor's overall teaching?
   (7-point scale: Very Poor-Superb)
2. How much have you learned as a result of this course?
   (7-point scale: Very Little-A Tremendous Amount)

Purdue University

CAFETERIA Core Items (5-point scale: Strongly Agree-Strongly Disagree)
1. My instructor motivates me to do my best work.
2. My instructor explains difficult material clearly.
3. Course assignments are interesting and stimulating.
4. Overall, this course is among the best I have ever taken.
5. Overall, this instructor is among the best teachers I have known.

specific department), and specific diagnostic items (Numbers 12 through 16) selected by the instructor.

Technical Quality

The technical quality of student ratings encompasses both the reliability and validity of ratings.

Reliability. Reliability refers to the extent the employed measurement procedures provide information that is free

TABLE 4.4   Generalizations about Reliability of Student Ratings

1. Student agreement on global ratings is sufficiently high if the class has over fifteen students. (41, 56, 57, 96, 99)
2. Students are consistent in their global ratings of the same instructor at different times in the course. (27)
3. An instructor's overall teaching performance in a course can be generalized from ratings from five or more classes taught by the instructor in which at least fifteen students were enrolled in each class. (41, 82)
4. The same instructor teaching different sections of the same course receives similar global ratings from each section. (125, 137)

from biases due to sampling of students, courses, and time of administration. There are two different types of reliability that are relevant to examining the trustworthiness of student ratings.

(1) Agreement: The extent of agreement among students within a class rating the instructor and course.
(2) Stability: The extent to which the same students using the same student rating form would rate the instructor and course similarly at two different times.

A summary of generalizations based on the research on the reliability of student ratings is presented in Table 4.4. For a different conceptualization of reliability of student ratings using generalizability theory, see Doyle (1983), Crooks and Kane (1981), Gillmore, Kane, and Naccarato (1978), and Kane, Crooks, and Gillmore (1976).

The reliability of data obtained from rating scales is dependent on the type of item used in the student rating form (see Table 4.5 third column). Because higher reliability is recommended for personnel decisions, each item type is not equally appropriate for personnel purposes. Global items are the preferred type for personnel decisions whereas specific diagnostic type items, even though their reliability is lower, are recommended for improvement due to their increased informational value.

Validity. The other major aspect of technical quality is validity; that is, do ratings measure what they are intended to

TABLE 4.5 Reliability of Different Types of Ratings Scale Items

Type	ICES Examples	Reliability*	Reliability Quality Rating
A. Global	• Rate the Instructor (Excellent-Very Poor; 6-point scale)	• Results from a typical single class: range .8 to .9 for a single item (12, 41)	High
	• Rate the Course in General (Excellent-Very Poor; 6-point scale)	• Average for four sets of results from one instructor: range .8 to .9 for a single item (41)	High
B. General Concept (Dept. "Core")	• The instructor seemed well prepared for classes (Yes, always-No, seldom; 5-point scale)	• Results from a typical single class: range around .8 for five items calculated as a subscore (12, 41)	High
	• The course was (Organized-Disorganized; 5-point scale)	• Average for four sets of results from one instructor: range around .8 for five items calculated as a subscore (41)	Fairly High
C. Specific (Instructor-Selected)	• How often did the instructor review material? (Too much-Not enough; 5-point scale)	• Results from a typical single class: range of .6 to .8 for a minimum of five items calculated as a subscore (12, 41)	Moderate
	• How beneficial were the homework assignments? (Very beneficial-Just busy work; 5-point scale)	• Average for four sets of results from one instructor: range of .5 to .8 for five items calculated as a subscore (41)	Moderate to Low

*All results assume a class size of twenty students and apply to classes in general. Results may be somewhat higher or lower for any single class under consideration. The numbers in parentheses refer to the references included in the bibliography at the end of this guidebook.
SOURCE: Measurement and Research Division, University of Illinois at Urbana-Champaign.

TABLE 4.6 Factors Influencing Student Ratings of the Instructor or Course

Factor	Effect*	Recommendation for Use
1. Administration		
a. Student anonymity	Signed ratings are more positive than anonymous ratings (55, 142)	Students should remain anonymous
b. Instructor in classroom	If the instructor remains in the room, ratings are more positive	Instructor should leave classroom
c. Directions	If stated use is for promotion, ratings are more positive than if for improvement (30, 55)	Indicate which items are used for which purpose
d. Timing	Ratings administered during final exam are generally lower than those given during semester (64)	Administer during last two weeks of class and not last day of class or during final exam
e. Midterm	Unreliable if students can be identified	Use objective items only anonymously collected
2. Nature of Course		
a. Required/ elective	Students in elective courses give higher ratings than in required courses (13, 57)	Campus norms may partially account for status
b. Course level	Students in higher level courses tend to give higher ratings than in lower level (57, 96)	Required/elective norms may partially correct for this
c. Class size	Students in very small (under 10) and very large (over 150) courses tend to give higher ratings than students in the other courses (34, 57, 99)	Should be taken into account, if classes are small, administer surveys in every course.
d. Class size (fewer than six students)	Usually high ratings (41)	Use cautiously for personnel decisions
e. Discipline	Lower ratings are given in courses in science and highest ratings are in courses in Applied Life Studies and Education (34, 108)	Use both university and department norms and department core items if available.
3. Instructor		
a. Rank	Professors receive higher ratings than teaching assistants (13, 34, 94)	Campus norms may paritally account for rank (e.g., professorial and TA)
b. Sex of instructor	Inconsistent results (8, 60, 103)	Generally not needed to be taken into account
c. Personality characteristics	Warmth, enthusiasm are generally related to ratings of overall teaching competence (59)	Not to be used for personnel decisions

TABLE 4.6   Continued

Factor	Effect*	Recommendation for Use
d. Years teaching	Ratings of instructors increase during first 10 to 12 years of teaching and decline somewhat thereafter (27)	Needs to be considered with type of course taught
4. Student		
a. Expected grade	Students in classes with higher expected grades give higher ratings than those in classes with lower expected grades (27, 54)	Interpretation is difficult. High ratings might be a "reward" for an expected easy grade, but they may also mean that good grades are expected because much has been learned from a good teacher.
b. Prior interest	Prior interest generally is associated with higher ratings (95, 116, 118)	Confounded with many other factors, and thus difficult to interpret
c. Major/minor	Majors tend to give more positive ratings than non-majors (57)	Needs to be considered in assessing competence for personnel decisions
d. Sex	Small effects, but complex relationships have been obtained (8)	Complexity of the relationship prevents any trustworthy conclusions
e. Personality characteristics	No meaningful and consistent relationships (2)	Does not need to be considered for personnel decision
5. Instrumentation		
a. Placement of items	Specific items placed before global items has a minimal effect on overall ratings (117)	Global items can be placed at either the beginning or end of a survey
b. Number of response alternatives	Six point response scales yield higher item reliabilities than **five point response scales** (100, 108)	Global items should use more than five point response scales
c. Negative wording of items	Overall ratings of the course and instructor are not significantly affected by the number of negatively worded items (117)	Both negatively and positively worded items can be used
d. Labeling all scale points versus labeling only end points	Labeling only end points yields slightly higher means (65)	Response format used should be consistent for all items

*Numbers in parentheses refer to references at the end of this guidebook.

measure? Validity of ratings takes into account two issues: (1) To what extent do factors not under the control of the instructor bias student ratings? (2) Do student ratings correlate with other measures considered to be defensible indicators of effective instruction?

Research on factors influencing student ratings but not under the control of the instructor is voluminous. Unfortunately, the results are not always consistent and the interactive effects of the factors need to be taken into consideration. However, some generalizations are worth noting and are summarized in Table 4.6. These generalizations are particularly relevant for personnel decisions, because an instructor using evaluation for self-improvement can easily collect more information or regard the collected information as a warning of potential problems.

Given these generalizations, it is prudent to interpret student ratings of the instructor and course with an understanding of the contextual factors that may influence the ratings. For example, students may give low ratings to some courses in a department regardless of the instructor. In addition, several factors can be confounded that interfere with any clear interpretation of the influence of any one factor. For example, teaching assistants may be teaching more required and larger classes than senior faculty, and thus teaching assistants receive lower ratings because of the confounding effects of at least three factors: required/elective status of the course, rank of instructor, and class size.

Several generalizations can be made about the second issue of the relationship between student ratings and other measures or indicators of teaching competence. These generalizations, displayed in Table 4.7, point to two major themes: First, student ratings correlate with other measures of teaching competence, and thus they have sufficient validity to warrant their use for both personnel decisions and improvement purposes. Second, global ratings by students correlate more highly with student learning than do diagnostic ratings. Therefore, global ratings are recommended for personnel decision making.

TABLE 4.7   Relation Between Student Ratings and Other Measures
of Effective Instruction

High Positive Correlations Between . . .
   1. Student and alumni ratings of overall instructor competence. (32, 124)

Moderate Positive Correlations Between . . .
   2. Student overall ratings of instructor and student learning. (20, 37)
   3. Student overall ratings of the course and student learning. (20, 37)
   4. Student learning and student ratings of teaching skills of instructor. (37)
   5. Student overall ratings of instructor and instructor overall self-ratings. (11, 20, 47, 98)
   6. Student overall ratings of instructor competence as measured by ratings, written comments to open-ended questions, and interviews. (122)

Low Positive Correlations Between . . .
   7. Student learning and student ratings of student/teacher interaction, feedback, and evaluation. (37)
   8. Student learning and student ratings of course structure and organization. (20, 37)
   9. Student ratings of course difficulty and ratings of instructor's teaching skill. (37)

Low Negative Correlations Between . . .
   10. Student ratings of course difficulty and student ratings of course structure and instructor-student report. (63)

Negligible Correlations Between . . .
   11. Student ratings of course difficulty and student learning. (37)

NOTE: Numbers in parentheses refer to references at the end of this guidebook.

Using Normative Comparisons

Norms are used for two purposes. First, a reference group provides relative comparisons; that is, how an instructor is rated when compared to ratings of other instructors in the norm or reference group. Second, norms help interpret possible biases in ratings due to factors not under the control of the teacher. For example, in the ICES system separate comparison groups are developed for teaching assistants and professors and for classes students are required to take the class or enroll in as electives. In the IDEA system, norm groups take class size into account. By providing a number of different comparisons groups, the influence of the factors that define the norm groups can be taken into account.

Some questions about norms. A first question in assessing student rating normative data relates to appropriateness. Are norms necessary? Norms are necessary if comparative judgments are desired. If we want to know how well a teacher is rated relative to others, norms are needed. However, an over-reliance on norms can be ill-advised from a legal perspective. Just because a faculty member ranks below average, it does not necessarily follow that he/she is incompetent or not effective. Competence is to be judged by how well an instructor fulfills assigned responsibilities. In addition, by the very nature of norms, half the faculty are below average in any reference group. This added information may enhance interpretation but may lead to low faculty morale, discouragement, hostility, and even lower productivity. Finally, norms are considerably less important if student ratings are used for course improvement or instructor feedback. Instructors can best spend their time examining strengths and weaknesses and areas for improvement.

The second question relates to the appropriateness of the reference group used for comparison. Local norms are generally the most appropriate. At present, no norms representing the whole spectrum of higher education in this country exist. It would be futile to expect such norms and possibly misleading to apply them. At a local institutional level, norms still need to be examined for their representativeness. If a unique group of instructors (e.g., only those who choose to participate in an evaluation program) constitute the group, it may produce misleading comparisons.

The approach selected for ICES norms is consistent with our designation for use of results by item type. For *global* items, one norm table is constructed based upon two factors: instructor rank (teaching assistant versus other faculty) and the required-elective nature of the course (three categories; mostly required, mostly elective, and those in between). These two factors are used since they control potential biases more than other factors except for expected grade. Additionally, a second comparison is provided based on the academic discipline of the faculty user. For *general concept* items, comparisons are made with disciplinary user group; economics faculty, for example. For *specific* items, no norms are provided. Instead, a verbal interpretation of the mean (weakness, average, or strength) and a verbal interpretation of the standard deviation (low, average, or high agreement) is printed on the report. (See Appendix F for a facsimile of this reporting scheme.)

A third question centers on the stability or consistency of ratings. If each of two sets of ratings for a given instructor in consecutive years is similar in absolute value, the ranking in the reference groups should be also similar. The stability of the ICES *global* item "Rate the Instructor" for professors teaching elective, mixed, and required courses for the past five years is illustrated in Figure 4.1. Mean ratings on this item vary little from year to year, even though the overlap of instructors included in this group is no more than 75 to 80 percent and the number of instructors is close to one thousand per year for each subgroup.

The fourth question relates to interpretation of results. To take into account the unreliability of mean ratings, the relative placement of the mean and an error designation surrounding the mean can be displayed on a report. The error designation, based upon calculated reliability, is included as a caution. If item reliability is quite low, the error designation will be quite wide, and the user can conclude that the rating should be interpreted very cautiously. A facsimile for ICES global item results is given in Appendix F to illustrate this display.

Suggestions for Using Student Ratings

The purpose (use) of the evaluation needs to first be determined, since the purpose influences the type of student rating items to be selected. Although the dual purposes of self-improvement and personnel decisions can lead to conflicts, a strategy can be designed whereby many of potential conflicts can be alleviated, if not eliminated. This strategy is outlined in Table 4.8. It is based on the principle that dif-

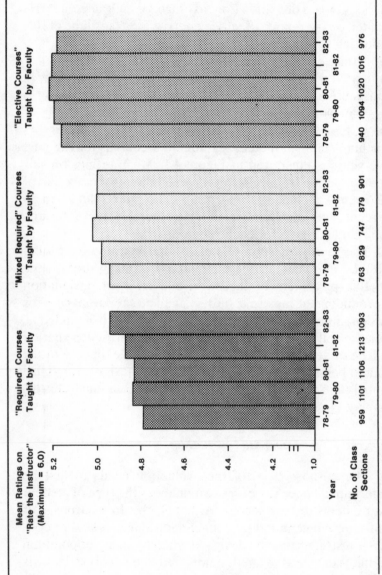

Figure 4.1 Faculty Mean Ratings for the ICES Global Item "Rate the Instructor" by Norm Category for Five Years

50

TABLE 4.8   Item Type and Usefulness

Item Type	Usefulness for Personnel	Usefulness for Improvement	Recommended Distribution To
1. Global			
Rate the course content	Good	Poor	Instructor, depart-
Rate the instructor	Very Good	Poor	mental administrator,
Rate the course in			and promotion/tenure
general	Very Good	Poor	committees
2. General Concept	Good	Good	Instructor and to other others depending on department policy
3. Specific, Diagnostic	Poor	Very Good	Instructor only

SOURCE: Measurement and Research Division, University of Illinois at Urbana-Champaign. Used by permission.

ferent types of items are best used for different purposes. If both types of items are included in a single form, then both purposes can be met.

For Personnel Decisions

(1) Student ratings should not be the sole piece of evaluative information as a basis for judging instructor competence.

(2) Global ratings are more appropriate than highly diagnostic items to evaluate overall instructor competence or the course in general.

(3) Requiring student ratings of every course every semester may result in overkill, because students may not take the evaluation seriously. Rather, a random or representative selection of courses is recommended, especially for faculty who have earned tenure.

(4) Students should be informed if the ratings are to be used for personnel purposes.

(5) Survey forms administered sometime during the last two or three weeks of the semester (or quarter) are preferred to administration immediately after or during the final exam period.

(6) Instructors may distribute the form and use a standard set of directions. It is recommended that they then leave immediately and provide at least ten minutes of class time for the students to complete the form. A student can collect the

forms and place them in campus mail to a central office for processing.

(7) The credibility of infomation is tied to the proportion of students completing the survey. At least 80 percent of the students should be available on the day the student surveys are completed.

(8) Student evaluation forms should not be returned to the instructor until after the final grades have been submitted so that students do not perceive any threat of retaliation from the instructor.

(9) A department may wish to establish a departmental core (i.e., a set of items used by all departmental faculty) to make additional comparisons among the faculty in a department. Since core items are normed for each department, comparisons within a department can be obtained for these items as well as for the global items. Generally, this type of comparison is possible with both cafeteria and omnibus forms.

(10) At least five sets of evaluations, each based on at least fifteen enrolled students, are recommended before student ratings are to be used for major personnel decisions. If the average number of students is ten or less, the number of evaluations should be at least eight. If ratings are given in every course every semester, a small number of items may be sufficient. More items can result in overkill, with students reducing their seriousness in responding and administrators receiving redundant information.

(11) A profile of student ratings, which includes item statistics such as means and standard deviations and normative comparisons, can serve as a cumulative record. Differences in student ratings due to such factors as class size and type of course can be noted by such a listing.

(12) If instructors are to be compared with others, factors out of the control of the instructor need to be taken into account in the interpretation of the ratings. Norms may help but they only provide a statistical basis to take into account general anomalies. Interpretation of normative (i.e., comparative) results still requires human judgment, since other factors not included in the norms may be important. Other

faculty who have first-hand experience with a course can generally provide additional information that can increase the accuracy of the interpretation of student ratings.

For Improvement

(1) Specific and diagnostic items are the most appropriate items, because they attempt to measure specific teacher behaviors or course characteristics.

(2) The variability of responses to each item (as denoted by the frequency of responses to each alternative and the standard deviation) can be as informative as the central tendency of responses (as denoted by the mean—the arithmetic average, or the median—the point at which one half of the scores are above and below).

(3) A particular area or problem with instruction can be investigated by selecting a number of specific items pertaining to that area or problem. However, one caution should be noted: If instructors concentrate solely on weaknesses, then students may be more negative about the course in general than if a more balanced set of items is selected.

(4) Student ratings given early—for example, midterm—can be used to make changes during the current semester. However, if instructors receive feedback before grades are determined, they need to regard feedback as constructive criticism and try not to let negative comments adversely affect the working relationship between them and the students. Instructors, by discussing the evaluation with students in class, can respond to criticisms and also demonstrate to the students that their feedback is being taken seriously.

(5) Student responses to specific and diagnostic items are recommended to be sent only to the instructor and not be distributed to others without the consent of the instructor.

(6) The ratings may be more fully utilized if the instructor works with a faculty colleague or a professional staff member responsible for faculty development. The instructor can learn ways to change and improve as well as discuss the results in a supportive atmosphere. A colleague who serves as a counselor generally should not also be responsible for

making personnel decisions, since this may result in a serious conflict of roles. Openness and trust are essential for a serious examination of strengths and weaknesses.

B. WRITTEN APPRAISALS

Student written comments to open-ended questions are used extensively by faculty, primarily for examining strengths and weaknesses of their courses and their instructional style. Students can be asked to comment about specific components of a course or about the course in general. The questions can be about assessments of current practices or suggestions for improvement. Written comments are considered one of the most useful types of information to faculty in revising their courses and their teaching style.

Examples. Developing a set of open-ended questions is a relatively easy task. They can be written on chalkboard, plain sheets of paper, or included as part of the student rating form. Open-ended questions are often included as part of a student rating survey. (See Appendixes A-E for some examples.)

The questions are usually quite general in scope. They give students opportunities to express their most salient opinions. Some sample question examples include the following:

(1) What are the major strengths of the instructor?
(2) What do you suggest to improve this course?
(3) How could the instructor improve as a teacher?
(4) What did you like best about this course?
(5) What topics do you consider to be the most useful in your education?

Another strategy for collecting written student opinions about courses and instructors is a mock letter of recommendation. In his classes, Dr. Alan Purves, Professor of Elementary Education at the University of Illinois at Urbana—Champaign, asks students to write a mock letter to a fellow student interested in taking the same course and instructor the following semester. In an one-page letter, students are asked to comment about specific components of the course as well as the course as a whole. The letter should conclude with a recommendation for others to enroll in or avoid the course.

Technical Quality

Student written comments as one form of evaluative information has been studied for its usefulness and credibility. The generalizations based on research are presented in Table 4.9.

Suggestions for Using Written Appraisals

Student written comments are best used for improvement purposes. Written comments about specific aspects of a course or teaching strategy are especially helpful to gain a flavor of the course from the student's perspective. If written comments are used for personnel decisions, they need to be used judiciously. Some suggestions are listed below.

For Personnel Decisions

(1) All comments from all students are seldom practical to record and transmit to another person.

(2) A random sample of comments can be used to counteract bias in selection. If used, the sample should be identified as such.

(3) A summarization of the comments should be done by someone other than the instructor being evaluated.

(4) Comments from students in very small classes generally need to be interpreted within the context of the small class size.

For Improvement

(1) Student comments can be requested at any time during the semester and can be done frequently, but precautions such as anonymity and the instructor's ability to treat negative remarks constructively are necessary.

TABLE 4.9   Generalizations about the Technical Quality of
Student Written Appraisals

1. Student written comments to open-ended questions are diverse and include comments about both the instructor and the course. (26)
2. Students tend to focus their comments on instructor characteristics (enthusiasm, rapport) and what they learned rather on the organization and structure of the course. (26)
3. Students give few detailed suggestions about how to improve a course. They are better critics than course designers. (26)
4. Faculty regard student written comments as less credible than student responses to global items when the information is for personnel decisions. Faculty regard written comments as more credible when the purpose was self-improvement. (121)
5. Global overall ratings of the instructor and course based on student responses to scaled items, written comments, and student interview are similar. Thus the method of collecting information does not influence student evaluations of the overall teaching competence of an instructor or the quality of the course. (122)

NOTE: Numbers in parentheses refer to references at the end of this guidebook.

(2) If an instructor desires information about a specific feature of the course, the question should be worded appropriately.

(3) Some students may get very personal and critical in their comments, so an instructor needs to be prepared to deal with all kinds of responses.

(4) Students are better at writing *what* they liked or disliked and considered to be worthwhile/worthless that analyzing *why* or at making suggestions for improving the course structure or teaching style.

(5) It is not recommended that students be asked to include their names on the evaluation. Students also may be reluctant to be candid if they think their identity can be determined by their handwriting style.

(6) An instructor needs to view written appraisals as constructive criticism and consider the potential impact of negative comments on the student-instructor relationship if comments are collected during the semester.

(7) An instructor can prevent unnecessary bias by reading the final student evaluations after he or she submits the course grades.

(8) Discussion of the student comments with another faculty member or a staff member responsible for faculty development can be very helpful in isolating problems and suggestions for improvement.

C. INTERVIEWS

An interview with enrolled students can be used to provide information about the course and the instructor's teaching style. Interviews can be conducted individually or in groups and the interviewer can be a faculty colleague or a professional staff member responsible for faculty development.

The interview can be highly structured, semistructured, or unstructured, and the purpose could be for personnel decision or improvement.

A group interview is recommended if the instructor wishes to learn how students react to a specific aspect of the course. If the interview is properly handled, students have considerable freedom to express their views and the interviewer has the opportunity to pursue topics and concerns brought up in the interview. Thus an interviewer can uncover unusual strengths and weaknesses as well as contrast student verbal comments with evaluations obtained by other methods such as rating scales and written comments.

Although the interview has several advantages, the cost of interviewing is substantial relative to student ratings or written appraisals. Individual interviews are especially expensive because of their labor intensity. Thus interviewing is seldom a routine way to gain information from students about each individual class taught by an instructor.

Technical Quality

Generalizations regarding the technical quality of group interviews are presented in Table 4.10.

Suggestions for Using Student Interviews

There are several ways group interviews can be conducted. Two of the most common both involve someone other than the instructor being in charge of a twenty- to

TABLE 4.10   Generalizations about the Technical Quality
of Student Interviews

1. Global overall ratings of the instructor and course based on student responses to scaled items, written comments, and student interviews are similar. Thus the method of collecting information does not influence student evaluations of the overall teaching competence of an instructor or the quality of the course. (122)
2. Student interview summaries are rated as more trustworthy by faculty for promotion purposes than are student responses to global items and student written comments. (121)
3. Representativeness of student comments in the interview can be suspect if not all students participate in an interview and/or if individual students in a group dominate the interview and try to persuade others to go along with their views. (42)

NOTE: Numbers in parentheses refer to references at the end of this guidebook.

thirty-minute interview conducted during the class time. In one approach, the interviewer (either a colleague or staff member responsible for faculty development) organizes students into small groups of five to six, asks each group of students to decide on strengths and weaknesses of the course, and to make suggestions. This can be done in approximately ten minutes. In the latter part of the session, the evaluator collects information from each group and summarizes the major themes, asking the groups to help form a consensus of opinion. The evaluator writes a summary and shares the written report with the instructor. (See Clark & Bekey, 1979, for a more complete description.) In a second group interview approach, all students in a class are interviewed as one group. One person conducts the interviews, while another person records the comments. Suggestions for conducting this type of interview are listed in the section on using student interviews "For Improvement."

Individual interviews with students have been used in personnel decisions. At Augustana College, a small liberal arts college in Illinois, faculty during their promotion year are asked to provide a list of ten seniors "who could provide a fair evaluation of the instructor's classroom and laboratory performance." Similarly, each tenured faculty member in the instructor's department is also asked to provide a list of ten students whose opinion they value regarding departmental instruction. Students are interviewed by the chairperson of the promotion review committee using the structured interview schedule presented in Appendix G. Students are also asked to complete a brief written questionnaire after the interview. This latter information is used primarily as a check against the interview data and any major discrepancies are noted. After all the interviews have been conducted, the department chair occasionally reinterviews several of the students to check the accuracy of the interpretation presented in the written summaries of the initial interviews.

For Personnel Decisions

(1) The information obtained from an interview is qualitative and difficult to summarize in numerical terms. Thus its use for personnel evaluations is most appropriate when an in-depth review and analysis of the instructor's effectiveness is needed.

(2) Students should be informed of the purpose of the interview.

(3) If several groups are interviewed, an interview schedule can ensure uniformity of procedures.

For Improvement

(1) The interviewer(s) can be faculty colleagues or professional staff responsible for faculty development. The interview is a good initial step in an ongoing process of change and development.

(2) The interviewer(s) can benefit by meeting with the instructor to discuss the instructor's goals for the course, perspective of the course, and potential problem areas, course requirements such as tests, and arrange for a follow-up session to the interview before the student interview is conducted.

(3) The interviewer(s) should develop and use a semi-structured interview schedule.

(4) If possible, one member of the team takes the lead in asking the questions while the other takes extensive notes. Since students' confidentiality needs to be protected, tape-recording the interview is unwise. The instructor also should not have access to interview notes (or tape recordings).

(5) Groups of ten to fifteen students are preferred. Interviewer(s) need to try to obtain comments from as many students as possible and not let vocal students dominate the input and tone of the interview. On getting a show of hands, the interviewer can obtain the degree of agreement or disagreement to an expressed opinion.

(6) At least twenty minutes are generally needed for a group interview. The instructor can introduce the interviewer(s) but is not to be present during the interview. The interviewer(s) can introduce themselves and inform students of the procedures to be used and the distribution of a subsequent report. Students arranged in a semi-circle or around a table often makes the interview more informal and conversational.

(7) The interviewer(s) prepares a one- to three-page written summary of each interview as a way to focus on the major points raised in the interview. The report should be diagnostic and descriptive in style; impressions of the interviewer are to be clearly identified as such.

(8) The interviewer(s) can maximize the value of the interview by meeting with the instructor as soon as possible to discuss the interview summary and to discuss alternative teaching practices.

D. TESTS OF ACHIEVEMENT

Most faculty consider student achievement as the most defensible criterion for assessing the competence of an instructor and/or the attainment of the course learning objectives. Unfortunately, achievement tests, homework assignments, or course grades are seldom used as indicators or measures of teaching competence. Their lack of use is due to tradition and to interpretation problems.

Technical Quality

Measures of student achievement, when used as criteria for assessing instructor competence also are to be appropriate, valid, reliable, and fair. An *appropriate* measure assesses student outcomes that are intended to be affected by classroom instruction. For example, an instructor should not be judged by his/her students' performance on a general achievement exam (e.g., CLEP). A *valid* measure assesses student performance on the specific goals and objectives of the course. A *reliable* measure produces similar results on different administrations. If scoring a test or assignment is not done with care, the results cannot be trustworthy. Finally, when comparisons are made among performances of students in different sections of the same course, a *fair* measure would not place any instructor of a course section at an advantage or disadvantage. For example, all instructors should have the same knowledge of and access to the test prior to its administration. Table 4.11 lists major ways in which student achievement can be judged. For a review of the use of student achievement in evaluating teacher effectiveness, see Millman (1981a).

Suggestions for Using Tests of Achievement

Student achievement can be an extremely important piece of information for an overall evaluation of an instructor if the display of test information is interpretable. Interpretation is dependent upon type of test employed and thus a description of the examination procedures and philosophy adopted by an instructor is essential to understanding the display of the achievement data.

TABLE 4.11 Three Major Ways of Judging Amount of Student Learning

1. Different instructors teaching the same course can be compared in terms of student performance on a common exam, provided the students in the classes are relatively comparable in ability, prior knowledge of subject matter, and motivation. Unfortunately seldom are all differences among students in various classes of little or no consquence. (35)
2. Pre- and postcourse test score differences can be used to obtain an index of learning. There is an obvious problem with this strategy. For example, an instructor could construct difficult precourse exams and easy post-course exams, which would result in large pre-post differences. (35)
3. A pre-established number of students in a course who answer correctly a specified percentage of test items; e.g., 75, 80, or 90 percent can be used as an indicator of student learning. (35)

NOTE: Numbers in parentheses refer to references at the end of this guidebook.

For Personnel Decisions

(1) Student performance on classroom exams is one important piece of evaluative information. Despite its intrinsic value as a criterion for evaluation, it seldom can be the sole criterion for assessing instructor teaching competence.

(2) Comparisons among performances of students in different sections of the same course are only valid if the course goals are specified, students are randomly assigned to each section, and testing conditions are constant for all students (e.g., identical tests, testing time).

(3) Absolute and relative evaluations of student performance should be clearly identified. If no comparisons can be made among different sections or classes, then judgments about achievement in a given class may require consultation with other colleagues familiar with the course content and types of students enrolled in the course.

For Improvement

(1) Frequent informal quizzes can be given as a check on progress for both the student and the instructor. This strategy also affects the study habits of some students, which

may be beneficial in courses where a consistent study pattern is needed.

(2) Information collected from students through the use of matrix sampling (not all students receive every item, but a portion of students receive a portion of the test items) can result in more coverage of the material for a given length of testing time. The tests can not be used for grading but total time spent taking exams by students is greatly reduced. For an exposition of matrix sampling, see Millman (1981a).

(3) As microcomputer hardware and software becomes readily available in higher education, the advantages of computer-assisted testing will become more prominent. Course improvement will become more feasible as this technology incorporates procedures, such as matrix sampling, for formative evaluation. Additionally, problem sets requiring tedious hand-grading in the past can now be handled more efficiently by computer, thus encouraging their maximum use in the classroom.

Section II: Colleagues as Sources

Colleagues include faculty peers, departmental administrators, and professional staff responsible for faculty development. Colleagues who have the necessary expertise in the discipline of the faculty member being evaluated are in an excellent position to judge

- instructor's knowledge and expertise in major field as reflected by the course syllabus and the reading list;
- instructor selection of realistic course objectives;
- instructor assignments, group projects, and examinations;
- student achievement as indicated by performance on exams and projects;
- contributions to instructional efforts in the department;
- thesis supervision;
- involvement in instructional research;

- student-instructor relations within the classroom; and
- instructor's style as a scholar and as a model teacher.

However, colleague evaluations of instructional competence must be done with considerable care and planning. A formal peer-evaluation program in which faculty in a department serve as evaluators can influence professional relationships and department collegiality as well as the relationship between departmental (college) leadership and faculty. Although faculty members may consider a formal system more fair than an informal one, they still may be reluctant to engage in an elaborate formal system of evaluation. If a pervasive judgmental climate emerges, it can be counterproductive. If faculty members think they are spending too much time evaluating others or are being continually evaluated, they may regard evaluation as an unnecessary intrusion on their time to carry out their responsibilities as scholars and teachers. Thus each departmental faculty needs to develop its own plan of colleague evaluation, and faculty involvement is necessary before a credible system is operative. (A plan of peer evaluation used by the Department of Horticulture at the University of Illinois at Urbana-Champaign is included in Appendix H.)

Colleagues who have the necessary expertise in the discipline of the faculty member being evaluated can provide useful evaluative information in three areas: (1) observations of the instructor in the classroom, (2) appraisal of course materials, and (3) evaluation of instructor in instructional development activities and advising.

A. CLASSROOM OBSERVATIONS

Classroom behavior is something that colleagues may choose to evaluate. Observations of classroom behavior are intended for evaluating the teaching process and its possible relationship to student learning. The focus is on the verbal and nonverbal behaviors of both the instructor and the students in the classroom. The effects of instruction such as student learning are not studied per se.

Of all the ways to collect evaluative information about teaching effectiveness, peer (faculty or administrator) visitation in the classroom is perhaps the most controversial. Its purported utility and appropriateness varies ranging from Michael Scriven's view that "it is a disgrace" (1981, p. 251) to others (e.g., French-Lazovik, 1981; Centra, 1975) who give cautions but positive support for this method of evaluating faculty teaching effectiveness.

Technical Quality

Generalizations regarding the technical quality of classroom observations are presented in Table 4.12.

Suggestions for Using Classroom Observations

Peer evaluations of a faculty member's classroom behavior can be based on checklists, rating scales, or written appraisals. Colleague written appraisals are open-ended and provide the best opportunity for a colleague not only to select what to observe or to judge but also how to interpret the information and structure the evaluation. Colleague observation is particularly appropriate for examining specific instructor behaviors of interest to the instructor. Peer evaluations are generally more appropriate for improvement purposes than for personnel decisions. Suggestions for each use are listed below.

For Personnel Decisions

(1) Those observing need to respect the instructor being evaluated. A faculty member with a strong difference of opinion or personal dislike for a colleague may have difficulty being fair.

TABLE 4.12   Generalizations about the Technical Quality of Classroom Observations

1. An observer may affect the teaching-learning process in the classroom. The instructor and students may act differently when an observer is present. (66)
2. Colleague ratings based on classroom observations are not highly reliable. Based on classroom observations, colleagues do not agree on an instructor's classroom instructional effectiveness. (31)
3. The relationship between observed instructor behavior in the classroom and student learning is not very strong. Certain instructional behaviors do not always result in increased student learning.
4. Colleague ratings are not highly related to student ratings of the instructor's effectiveness in the couse, if class time was well spent and if the instructor was open to other viewpoints. (31)
5. Colleagues and students reasonably agree on specific instructional practices. They agree on descriptions of activities but not on their judgments of instructional quality. (31)
6. Colleagues are more generous in their ratings than are students. Almost all colleagues rate their peers as excellent or good instructors.

NOTE: Numbers in parentheses refer to references at the end of this guidebook.

(2) Observations by more than one colleague are recommended, since colleagues—quite naturally—rely on their own experiences, values, and definitions of effective teaching in making evaluations. Cross-checking of interpretations and judgments is a good strategy for establishing reliable and credible information. Agreement may not be even possible or desired, since observers often vary in their definitions of effective instruction.

(3) At least three or four classroom observations for a given class over a single semester are needed to ensure adequate representation. An observation is suspect if only one classroom visit is made.

(4) Colleague judgments about classroom teaching style and relationships with students need to be used judiciously. A focus on substantive issues, such as sequence of topics, recency and accuracy of the content presented, scholarship, ethical and professional conduct such as racism or sexism seem the most appropriate.

(5) If different colleagues are writing appraisals based on observations, the areas to be evaluated should be agreed

upon in advance. The quality of teacher performance observed can be left to the discretion of each colleague conducting the observations.

(6) A summary of different colleague evaluations can be made to point out and possibly reconcile differences in observations and judgments.

For Improvement

(1) Colleague observations should not be the sole piece of information used in an evaluation.

(2) Faculty from similar academic disciplines can best assess an instructor's ability to present his/her scholarship to students, appropriate level of difficulty of material presented, relevance of examples, integration of topics, structure of the lecture, and congruence between instructor goals and accomplishments.

(3) During in-class observations, observers cannot simultaneously record every transaction or behavior. Thus, they need to focus on specific areas. Areas to observe include: (a) importance and suitability of content, (b) organization of content, (c) presentation style, (d) clarity of presentation, (e) questioning ability, and (f) establishing and maintaining contact with students.

(4) A method for recording the classroom observations is desirable. A rating of class behaviors rather than frequency of occurrence of specific behaviors is recommended. (Appendix I which presents a rating form of items classified into the areas listed in point 3 can be used by observers to focus their attention.)

(5) Faculty who trust and respect each other are necessary for open and honest exchange about strengths and weaknesses and possible ways to improve.

(6) Faculty members with considerable teaching experience and competence are generally the best evaluation consultants for instructional improvement purposes.

(7) A professional staff member responsible for faculty development can also be helpful by pointing out strengths

and weaknesses and discussing alternative ways of organizing the course and teaching skills.

(8) A colleague and the instructor should meet before the
initial observation is made. In this meeting the colleague can
receive copies of the course materials, learn the overall goals
of the course and the intent of the class period(s) to be
observed, discuss a method of observation, and arrange for
postobservation meetings. Observed instructors may also
suggest concerns and course dimensions on which they
would like feedback. A written appraisal of the observation
to be communicated to the instructor is most useful if it
included information about specific teaching behaviors, and
suggestions for alternative ways to improve teaching performance.

(9) A meeting following the observation is especially
valuable for discussing the observations.

(10) Video-taping classroom activity can often provide
instructors with an insightful portrayal of their teaching.
Video-taping, however, should be used cautiously because it
can be threatening (Fuller & Manning, 1973). Since the
medium focuses on the teaching performance and physical
appearance of the instructor, more than one video-taping
may be needed before an instructor can move away from a
concern over appearance and concentrate on the content of
the lecture and teaching skills.

(11) Colleague appraisal based on classroom observation
or videotape is especially useful in a continuous program of
evaluation for course improvement purposes. The issues of
confidentiality, authenticity of the behavior, obtrusiveness of
the observers, and subjectivity in evaluating classroom behaviors can more easily be dealt with if the instructor has the
opportunity to respond and discuss the peer evaluations.

B. REVIEW OF CLASSROOM MATERIALS

Faculty colleagues are especially useful in providing
evaluative information about an instructor's course syllabi,

assignments, testing and grading practices, text selection, and about students' achievements. Not only is this form of evaluation relatively nonthreatening to the instructor, but it properly uses the expertise of the faculty colleagues. Peers do not need to enter the classroom to conduct this evaluation, and they can do it in a relatively short period of time. A meeting with the instructor also allows instructors to explain their goals of the course, the type of students enrolled in the course, and special problems and constraints.

A variety of course materials can be evaluated by faculty peers. Appendix J presents a checklist organized into three areas—course organization; readings, projects, and laboratory assignments; and exams and grading. In our opinion, this strategy has not been practiced as much as it can be. A dialogue among instructors has special spinoffs, including some possible new insights into teaching for those doing the evaluating. A senior faculty member, with sufficient expertise in the course content and teaching experience, can assist younger faculty in areas like relevance, level of difficulty, and appropriateness of tests and assignments. This strategy can also be used for both personnel and improvement purposes. The review of the materials can be done for both uses; only the reporting needs to differ.

C. REVIEW OF INSTRUCTIONAL DEVELOPMENT AND ADVISING

Faculty colleagues are also in a good position to evaluate out-of-class activities such as instructional and curricular development, academic, vocational, or professional advising and instructional research. However, colleagues who evaluate a faculty member need more than second-hand knowledge to conduct a comprehensive evaluation. A checklist of items classified into four areas (colleagueship, participation in university community, vocational and personal advising, and academic and thesis advising) is presented in Appendix K. This can be used as a guide to obtain a comprehensive assessment of an instructor's involvement in out-of-classroom activities.

Section III: Self as a Source

Self-evaluations range from informal self-reflections to formal written appraisals penned for others. Instructors can benefit by systematically analyzing what and how they teach. Since a major goal of any evaluation program is to encourage faculty to become monitors of their own performance, self-evaluations provide opportunities for instructors to reflect upon their own teaching. Self-assessment can be both descriptive and judgmental. The following information is recommended for a self-evaluation:

- courses taught and enrollments;
- course materials, syllabus, and assignments;
- course objective and goals;
- course outcomes and student learning as measured by the exams and projects;
- advising responsibilities;
- involvement in curriculum projects;
- evaluations by colleagues; and
- special teaching methods and techniques tried as ways to improve teaching competence.

Technical Quality

The generalizations based on self ratings and evaluations are summarized in Table 4.13.

Examples. Self-evaluations can be accomplished in a number of ways. First, instructors can write their philosophy of teaching strategy and judgments of their strengths and weaknesses. Self-appraisal can often serve as the initial step in an ongoing attempt by instructors to improve. A written self-evaluation then becomes a part of an integrated self-appraisal that can include a description of the course objectives and goals, course syllabus, assignments, and method of teaching.

TABLE 4.13   Generalizations about the Technical Quality
of Self Evaluations

1. Students and instructors generally show good relative agreement on overall ratings of the instructor; i.e., instructors rated highly by students rate themselves higher than instructors rated less highly by students. (11, 20, 47, 98)
2. Instructor self and student ratings on specific dimensions of student involvement, teacher support, and instructional skill are the most congruent. (20, 94)
3. Instructor self ratings are not unduly influenced by the instructors's age, sex, tenure status, teaching load, or years of teaching experience. (48)

NOTE: Numbers in parentheses refer to references at the end of this guidebook.

Second, instructors can rate themselves on a set of items on a checklist or rating scale. A student rating form or catalog of items can be used for item generation. Items in Appendix I can be used if only classroom behavior is to be assessed. Third, instructors can use a form like the Instructor Self-Evaluation Form (ISEF) as in Batista and Brandenburg (1978). This survey, listed in Appendix L, consists of four scales: adequacy of classroom procedures, enthusiasm and knowledge for teaching, stimulation of cognitive and affective gains in students, and relations with students. Four items—one item from each scale—are presented in a set of forms. Instructors rank order the four items in terms of the items being most to least descriptive of their teaching. Because of this forced-choice, instructors are required to indicate their own relative strengths and weaknesses, and they can not specify strengths and weaknesses in some or all of the four areas represented by the scales. Thus this forced type of measurement may not accurately measure the absolute self-ratings of strengths and weaknesses; instead relative strengths are to be interpreted.

Suggestions for Using Self-Evaluations

The value of self-evaluations are highly dependent upon purpose. A statement of accomplishments and approach to teaching is ideal for course improvement. Almost without exception, it is the recommended first step in forming any formal or informal type of faculty growth contract (a strategic plan that includes the faculty member's goals, ways to accomplish them, and the needed resources). If such arrangements are used, then the faculty member's ability to assess his/her current status and exceptions is critical. This strategy depends on considerable communication between each faculty member and the administration, which then makes possible a discussion of the institutional's expectations, rewards, and available resources. (For more information on growth contracts, see Seldin, 1982).

Self-judgments of overall teaching competence used for personnel decisions are fraught with problems, most notably credibility. Self-assessment in the form of description of course materials and philosophy of teaching are often more acceptable than self-judgments of value or worth when used for personnel decisions. Thus self-evaluations are a critical piece of information for each purpose, but the type of information collected and communicated to whom should vary for intended use.

For Personnel Decisions

(1) Self-ratings of overall teaching competence are not recommended for personnel decisions. Instead, descriptions of teaching, philosophy, load, and strategy are preferred as input into the evaluation process.

(2) Self-evaluations of teaching provide contextual information for assessing teaching effectiveness for annual salary reviews. Descriptions of accomplishments and future goals can provide a useful framework for evaluating the total instructional performance of a professor.

For Improvement

(1) Self-ratings should be compared with ratings of students if the same items are administered to the students.

(2) Faculty can increase the utility of their self-evaluation by discussing the evaluation with faculty colleagues or a staff member responsible for faculty development.

(3) Instructors wishing to focus on specific classroom teaching behavior should consider videotaping a lecture or a discussion and using a self-administered rating scale such as the one presented for colleague review in Appendix E.

(4) If growth contracts are tried, self evaluation should be a key part in the success of contracts (Seldin, 1982).

Section IV: Alumni as Sources

Alumni and graduating seniors have a unique perspective to evaluate individual faculty, courses in their major field of study, and curricular offerings. Alumni have the additional advantage of being able to judge the relevance of their courses to their present job demands and expectations. Unfortunately, evaluations from graduating seniors and particularly alumni are relatively expensive to collect. Thus collecting evaluative information from these sources needs to be done after a comparison between need for the information and costs. Because of the lapse of time between a course and time of evaluation, assessments of highly specific aspects of a course or teaching style are generally not advocated. Instead, evaluations about the sequence and depth of course material and support and advice faculty gave to the students during their college career are valuable kinds of information to a department in its examination of its curriculum offerings and the role of its faculty in instruction.

Technical Quality

The research on the validity of alumni ratings is summarized in Table 4.14.

Suggestions for Using Alumni Evaluations

Collecting information from graduating seniors can be done by exit interviews, telephone, letters, and mail surveys, but only the last two are generally economically feasible for

TABLE 4.14   Generalizations about the Technical Quality
of Alumni Ratings

1. Students who have evaluated instructors twice (first during the course and then one year after graduation) show good absolute agreement; i.e., their ratings of the competence of the teacher was very similar. (125)
2. Alumni of five years or more and enrolled students show good relative agreement on their ratings of overall teaching effectiveness of instructors. (32)
3. Alumni ratings tend to be lower than ratings of enrolled students. (125)

NOTE: Numbers in parentheses refer to references at the end of this guidebook.

gathering information from alumni. Interviews with graduating seniors can provide considerable in-depth information about professors and courses, but this method is expensive. The logistical problems of having students come for an interview and the difficulty in summarizing interview data also need to be considered before the interview method is adopted.

Information requested by graduating seniors or alumni needs to be specified in the directions. If information about long-term comprehension and relevance of the content, personal development, technical skills, and motivation to learn is desired, questions about these areas need to be included in the directions.

For Personnel Decisions

(1) General items about instructor competence or course organization are preferred over detailed items about specific aspects of course.

(2) General items included in a rating form administered to enrolled students can be included in an alumni form if comparisons are desired.

(3) Someone other than the instructor needs to distribute the surveys, and the purpose for collecting the information must be made explicit to the alumni.

(4) Alumni having the option of returning surveys anonymously is preferred.

(5) Alumni should be given the opportunity to write comments on a mail survey.

(6) Alumni should be asked questions that take advantage of their perspective, such as relevance of course to current position, job demands, and suggestions for topics to be covered or relevance to their role in society.

(7) Alumni with varying years of work experience can often provide some interesting insights into the role of their collegiate education in their professional and personal lives.

(8) If several faculty are to be evaluated in a single administration, listing names of the instructors reduces biases due to name recall.

(9) Questions regarding the department/curriculum can easily be added to an alumni survey.

(10) If the response rate is low, for instance, under 50 percent, generalizations must be made cautiously. The available information may be quite biased—too positive or too negative.

(11) Instructors who teach a large number of students are likely to receive many positive *and* negative comments about their teaching.

For Improvement

(1) Since diagnostic information about specific components of a course is difficult to obtain from alumni, instructors are likely to be disappointed if they expect detailed critiques and specific suggestions for improvement.

(2) Alumni may point out deficiencies that have been corrected.

(3) Comparisons of alumni and enrolled student evaluations can be examined for common themes and differences.

Section V: Records as Sources

Records include grade distributions of students enrolled in courses, number of students enrolled in courses the first week and at end of semester, committee assignments, teaching load, types of course taught such as departmental core courses, generation of instructional units, student credit hours, advising loads, and so on. Some information can be obtained from faculty annual review reports; information such as grade distributions can often be obtained from reports issued by a central administration office, whereas other information is often contained in department records.

Suggestions for Using Records

(1) A record of teaching workload over a number of years (e.g., three to five years) provides a better portrayal of a professor's efforts and contributions than a record of the latest year. A long-range perspective helps interpret the contributions of a professor with an unusual teaching load.

(2) Comparisons of first week and final course enrollment can be helpful in pointing out unusual large decreases in number of students throughout the semester (as compared to others teaching the same course). This information can serve as a warning flag in interpreting end-of-course student ratings as well as a topic of discussion with the instructor regarding the reasons for dramatic enrollment shifts. Interpretation should be made cautiously, however, since students drop courses for several reasons and some may have little relevance to the instructor or course.

(3) Grade distributions can be used to detect unusual grading practices by the instructor. Comparisons with other instructors teaching the same or similar courses can be used in interpreting grading practices. Again caution should be used in inferences about instructor effectiveness on the basis of grades. Instructors who have honors classes or grade according to an established set of standards may have unique but defensible grade distributions.

CHAPTER 5

USING EVALUATIVE INFORMATION

Evaluative information is collected to be used. Thus considering use after the information is collected is, unfortunately, too late. As a working strategy, determining use should preceed information collection. Since use is related to the purpose to be made of the evaluation, use is one of the two overriding principles of our view of faculty evaluation. The other is that multiple perspectives are needed.

What Is Use?

We define use in a very broad sense to emphasize its importance. In Table 5.1 six phases of use are described. They begin with the user having the information available and end by having the use taking some form of action. This sequence is not strictly temporal. Going back and forth among the phases is recommended. Some comments about these phases are worth noting.

(1) Summarizing data involves cross-checking if a multiple perspective approach to evaluation is undertaken. The information collected from the various sources by different methods should first be cross-checked for patterns, inconsistencies, and for detection of unique strengths and glaring problems. Often one single theme is not possible; rather a

TABLE 5.1   Phases in Using Evaluative Information

* Having available the collected evaluative information (evidence, data)

* Summarizing and analyzing the information
  • reducing the raw data
  • • calculating statistical summaries of numerical data
  • deriving themes from qualitative data (e.g., interviews, written summaries)
  • cross-checking the various pieces of information

* Interpreting the information
  • weighting the relative importance of various pieces of information
  • assessing the credibility, validity, reliability, and meaning of the information
  • determining the worth and merit of the teaching performance

* Communicating the evaluation results (descriptions and judgments of worth and/or merit) to the appropriate parties

* Using the information for
  • enlightenment
    —new insights
    —new understandings
    —concerns for discussion and further review
  • decisions and actions
    —allocations of annual salary increases
    —promotion and tenure decisions
    —changes in teaching style and course
  • statisfying formal bureaucratic rules and regulations
  • justification for previous decisions

composite portrayal filled with an array of impressions, generalizations, and inferences is more accurate.

(2) Interpreting the data includes weighting. Each piece of information needs to be weighed in terms of its importance in determining a summative evaluation of an instructor. This weighting process is one of the most critical phases in an evaluation. Unfortunately, few explicit guidelines can be written, since this is heavily based on the professional judgments of those faculty, colleagues, and administrators examining the information. This weighting process, however, need not be secretive and done without a rationale. (One process for determining weights is described in Ory, 1980b).

One of the best strategies in weighting information is by the use of a set of accepted prescribed weights. This can be

TABLE 5.2   A Weighting Scheme for Evaluating Faculty
            for Annual Reviews

Area of Responsibility	Total Points	Source		
		Students	Peers	Self
Instruction	70			
Classroom performance	40	20	15	5
Advising	20	15		5
Course development	10		5	5
Service	10		5	5
Research	10		10	
Professional development	10		5	5
Totals	100	35	40	25

done by having faculty and administrators establish as policy the importance to be given to each area or criteria and their measured indicators (e.g., student ratings of instruction) in determining faculty teaching competence. Thus weights given to each area are known to the faculty before evaluation takes place. Weights given to a faculty member's contributions in teaching, research, and service can be noted; for instance, teaching receives a weight of 60 percent, research 30 percent, and service 10 percent. The types of evaluative information (i.e., the measures) to be used as indicators of the criteria can be specified so that faculty know the information on which teaching effectiveness is to be assessed. The appropriate faculty committees and administrators ultimately use professional judgment in their overall summative evaluation, but faculty at least know the areas, criteria, and information to be used in the evaluation. In Table 5.2 a sample weighting scheme, adapted from a state college, is presented. In using these schemes, a false sense of objectivity can occur, however. The process becomes mechanical and looks objective; but this strength is also its weakness. Evaluation of professional people like faculty is too complex and subjective to have everything reduced to a number. (Additional examples of weighting systems used at community colleges, based on the Southern Regional Educational

Board's Faculty Evaluation Project, are presented in a chapter by Smith, 1983. Also see Miller, 1974, for other examples.)

(3) Interpreting also involves assessing merit and worth (Scriven, 1978). Since worth is more institutional dependent than merit, it often is assessed. Judging worth cannot be accomplished without institutional goals, expectations, and standards being incorporated into the evaluation.

(4) Communicating evaluative information is best viewed as an ongoing process, especially if the purpose is for improvement. In our opinion this phase is too often slighted. It has been suggested that one third of all the effort in evaluation should be communication and discussion—a dialogue among the appropriate parties. If this were done, mutual problem solving and improvement may very likely be the beneficiaries of evaluation.

(5) Use is variously defined, as shown in Table 5.1. It is more than a hammer that needs pounding once in a while (Weiss, 1982). Use is best viewed not as a distinct phase of evaluation, separate from planning or from collecting and analyzing data. Instead, use can provide the direction to evaluation. Use involves reflection as well as decision making. Furthermore, not all uses are equally justifiable. If evaluation is undertaken to meet a rule or policy—to adhere to the letter of a law—its potential for constructive use is not very high. If evaluation is used or perceived to be employed as a cover for those in authority to justify a prior decision, evaluation will have a tarnished and counterproductive image.

In sum, using evaluation is something that needs attention. Without conscious effort to use evaluative information, evaluation does not reach its potential. A number of generalizations and suggestions related to enhancing use and developing a viable evaluation program are presented in Table 5.3.

TABLE 5.3   Generalizations about Enhancing the Usefulness of Evaluation

1. A consultive relationship between the instructor and another trusted colleague enhances the use of the information collected, because the information and possible future directions can be discussed. (38, 53, 79, 131)
2. An evaluation often points to problem identification rather than problem solution, and thus should be considered one part of a continous process of examination, adaptation, improvement, and evaluation.
3. Information is most useful if it focuses on behaviors and practices over which the instructor has some control.
4. Specific goals for improvement should be set based on the evaluative information received. (88)
5. How evaluative information is communicated can be as important as the content of the information.
6. If faculty are expected to improve their teaching style and behavior, they need alternatives and suggestions about how to improve. (105)
7. Descriptive information is often less threatening than evaluative judgments and opinions. (131)
8. Faculty may carry with them a long time the sting of a negative evaluation. (21)
9. In the early years of their career, faculty often rely on external feedback to form their professional self identity whereas in the latter years, external feedback is more often used to validate or question their self perceptions. (21)
10. Faculty do not equally rate all types of information as equally credible for all purposes. They prefer student written comments for learning about their teaching for improvement, but regard data from scaled objective items as more appropriate information for promotion and tenure decision. (121)
11. Instructors, especially those in their early careers, regard an annual meeting with an administrator (department chair, head, dean, vice president) to be very influential in learning and assessing their professional progress and status. (21)
12. Faculty and administrators as potential users of information often attach credibility to the contents of the information depending upon the source.
13. Too much information can be as much a problem as too little. Information not well synthesized is frustrating to a reader.
14. Decision making in universities and colleges is primarily shared decision making and thus evaluative information may be used differently at different levels of the organization.
15. A systematic program of evaluation of faculty is more than a management information system, because the focus is value, worth, merit, and effectiveness and an interactive communication network among the parties (faculty and administrators) is a crucial part of an evaluation program. (115)
16. Ownership of the evaluation program increases acceptance and credibility. Thus faculty and administrators who get involved in all phases of evaluation are more apt to use evaluation constructively.
17. Evaluation without apparent contingencies to those being evaluated soon reaches a point of diminishing returns. Thus evaluation can be more useful if it leads to ways of trying new teaching strategies and/or tied to the institution's reward system.
18. Potential users who have a perceived need for evaluative information more frequently use evaluative information than those who do not.
19. The potentiality of being evaluated may change how faculty behave in anticipation of the evaluation. For some, the threat value of an ensuing evaluation is high.

(continued)

TABLE 5.3   Continued

20. Formal evaluative information is generally given more attention when the users cannot rely on their own experiential knowledge.
21. Active administrative support, especially by the top level administration on a campus, is important for a successful evaluation program.
22. If no evaluation program currently exists on a campus, establishing a formal evaluation program is best done incrementally and with patience.
23. It is better to have an appropriate answer to the right question than a certain answer to the wrong quesion. (127)
24. Evaluation of one's worth or merit is often a deeply personal matter, and thus respect for privacy, acceptance of one's apprehension, denial and evasion as well as satisfaction, elation and even arrogance is sometimes needed.

Three Distinct Uses of Evaluation

Much of accumulating and summarizing information for assessing teaching effectiveness in higher education can be classified into three major uses. Information is collected and summarized for judging

- teaching effectiveness of an instructor in a specific course or the course in general,
- teaching effectiveness of a faculty member for annual faculty salary adjustments, and/or
- teaching effectiveness of a faculty member for promotion and/or tenure review.

Generally, the first use is for improvement, although the evaluation of an instructor's competence in teaching all his or her courses is often a personnel matter, as it should be.

SINGLE COURSE EVALUATIONS

Collecting information from various sources about a single course is ideal for cross-checking the evidence for patterns and dissimilarities. Integrating information from many perspectives also prevents undue importance to any one piece of information.

If the purpose of the evaluation is for improvement, a one-page summary of all the information available for a course can be constructed. Appendix M lists a form that is categorized around source (self, students, alumni, and peers) and major components of the course. It can be used to organize the synthesis of the available data as well as detect consistencies and conflicts. Instructors who complete this form for their own use should encounter few problems. If this form is used for personnel decisions, the credibility of this summarization can be increased easily by conducting a systematic analysis of the comments and by asking a colleague to verify the written summaries.

EVALUATIONS FOR ANNUAL SALARY ADJUSTMENTS

Faculty members often complete an annual report describing their accomplishments (usually in the areas of teaching, research, and service). Other information such as peer evaluations of instruction may be available to the administrators and committees responsible for making annual summative evaluations of the faculty.

Administrators, department heads/chairpersons, deans, and their respective advisory/executive committee use a variety of methods to obtain a composite overall evaluation of each faculty member. The following guidelines are given as guidance for assembling evaluative information about instructional performance.

Suggestions

(1) Since the importance given to accomplishments in teaching, research, and service is a part of determining a composite overall evaluation of a faculty member, weighting each area needs to be as explicitly spelled out as possible.

(2) The weights may include a range; for example, teaching performance is 40 to 60 percent of the typical faculty member's contribution. The weighting scheme should be sufficiently adjustable for any one faculty member to take into account unusual circumstances or contributions.

**TABLE 5.4   Proposed Plan for Evaluating Teaching
for Promotion and Tenure**

Type	Status	Source of Judgment	Recommended Format for Report
1. Global rating of instructor	Required	Students	Longitudinal Profile
2. Global rating of course	Required	Students	Longitudinal Profile
3. Ratings of components of a course	Optional	Students	Summary Profile
4. Course syllabi and materials	Recommended[a]	Students	Summary Profile
5. Student performance	Recommended[a]	Colleagues	Written Summary
6. Faculty contribution to course and curriculum development	Recommended[a]	Colleagues	Written Summary
7. Advising	Recommended	Colleagues	Written Summary
8. Awards	Required	Records	List

a. At least one of the types listed in 4, 5, or 6 is required.

NOTES: Information for assessing teaching effectiveness should include judgments from at least students and faculty peers. This chart lists the basic types of information that can be included in assessing instructional effectiveness of a faculty member for promotion/tenure.

1. *Global Rating of Instructor.* If normative information is to be presented a comparison group needs to be selected and identified in the interpretation. A profile of ratings for all (or selected) courses taught is preferred. See Appendix O for an example.

2. *Global Rating of Course.* The discussion about the instructor applies here.

3. *Ratings of Components of a Course.* The following topic areas can be used: general course organization, instructor-student relationships, course workload or difficulty, instructor communication skills, instructor's professional behavior, students' learning from the course, grading, and exams.

4. *Course Syllabus and Materials.* The documentation can include materials supplied by the instructor about his/her approach to teaching, variety of courses taught, and the number of students enrolled in the course. Course materials selected for review by faculty peers may include course syllabii, course objectives, sequence of topics, time and appropriateness of topics, reading lists, textbooks, audiovisual materials, homework assignments, laboratory work, projects, quality of examinations, and grading.

5. *Student Performance.* Colleague evaluations may include judgments about student performance as measured by their achievement tests, homework, laboratory work, and other assignments. Measures of assessment reviewed *must* be appropriate, valid, reliable, and fair. An analysis of student performance using assigned grades (or a comparison of grades with other classes) is not sufficient.

6. *Faculty Contribution to Course and Curriculum Development.* Colleagues may evaluate the faculty member's contribution in new course development, revisions of courses, services on department and other curriculum committees, development of new or revised programs or curricula, leadership in maintaining a viable curriculum, instructional research, consultation with other faculty on teaching and instruction, and use of innovating approaches to teaching.

7. *Advising.* An assessment of a professor's advising may include a professional contribution in academic advising (e.g., helping students on course selection, program of study, and career choices), thesis directorship, contribution on committees, spon-

TABLE 5.4 Continued

sorship of student organizations and student projects, and advising colleagues on instruction.
8. *Awards.* The listing of teaching and instructionally related awards may include those sponsored by the department, school, college or university, other awards sponsored by student groups, external agencies, professional societies.

multiple perspectives approach and offered as one version that can be adapted for local use.

Suggestions

Evaluative information about instruction for promotion/tenure can be useful if the following major guidelines are met.

(1) Information collected from various sources about a number of courses increases the comprehensiveness and fairness of the evaluation. Evaluations from only students or from only a few or the most recent courses taught by an instructor may present a biased view.

(2) It is recommended that a report of student ratings include the following information: title and name of course, number of students who returned survey, mean, and stan-

(3) A form to summarize the judgments based on the evaluative information can facilitate the review process. A form used by the Department of Business Administration at the University of Illinois at Urbana—Champaign is included in Appendix N. (This form is used for the evaluation of research and service as well.)

EVALUATIONS FOR PROMOTION AND TENURE REVIEW

Evaluation of instruction is almost without exception required in the promotion/tenure process. Since local policies and practices dictate procedures, only some general suggestions are presented here. We have included a suggested plan for evaluating teaching for promotion/tenure, which is presented in Table 5.4. This plan is based on the

dard deviation of an item, and an index of relative standing in a defined comparison group. Appendix O presents a profile of evaluations of all courses over a several year period taught by one professor at the University of Illinois at Urbana—Champaign who used ICES as the student rating form.

(3) Student responses to diagnostic items are seldom appropriate for inclusion in the documentation submitted for review by others.

(4) If student written comments are used, it is preferred that they be randomly selected. Themes and highlights presented without actual comments have low credibility, unless they are written or verified by a colleague.

(5) Colleague evaluations, if collected within a consultative arrangement for course improvement, are seldom justified for use in personnel decision making.

(6) Colleague and alumni information collected for personnel decisions may be shared with the instructor but disclosure to the instructor should not be required.

Conclusions

Evaluating is planning, collecting, analyzing, synthesizing, and using information to fulfill one or more purposes. To maximize the utility of evaluation, use is not to be considered some discrete add-on function after evaluation; rather it is an integral part of the process. Thus we have included it along with multiple perspectives as one of the two overriding principles in our view of evaluation of teaching effectiveness.

Given these emphases, evaluation is fundamentally a process—a practical, social, political, subjective, and human undertaking—as well as a technical, analytical procedure. In this process, we stress that defining good teaching, a necessary activity before evaluation of it can occur, is not easy. No one set of criteria or standard of excellence can apply to everyone. The judgment of the value (either merit, worth, or both) of a teacher can best be accomplished by employing a multiple perspectives approach.

We also stress that the best information (i.e., the most trustworthy, valid, efficient, feasible) should be collected and used for the purposes intended. Although we have divided purpose into personnel and improvement, these two functions are not necessarily independent and discrete. A good evaluation can meet both purposes in a complementary way.

Finally, use encompasses purpose and refers to many different activities, including allocation of resources, debate, decision, discussion, justification, problem identification, and understanding. Evaluative information can be appropriately used, misused, or not used. Merely fulfilling bureaucratic rules or collecting data that sits on a shelf is not sufficient.

In this guidebook we have presented generalizations, summaries, suggestions, forms, surveys, and techniques. We hope they will help, but in the end, the person doing the evaluation, either for himself or herself or for others, is the most significant.

STUDENT INSTRUCTIONAL REPORT

This questionnaire gives you an opportunity to express anonymously your views of this course and the way it has been taught. Indicate the response closest to your view by **blackening the appropriate circle**. Use a soft lead pencil (No. 2) for all responses to the questionnaire. Do not use a pen (ink, ball-point, or felt-tip).

SIR Report Number

SECTION I. Items 1-20. Blacken one response number for each question.

NA (0) = Not Applicable or don't know. The statement does not apply to this course or instructor, or you simply are not able to give a knowledgeable response.

SA (4) = Strongly Agree. You strongly agree with the statement as it applies to this course or instructor.

 A (3) = Agree. You agree more than you disagree with the statement as it applies to this course or instructor.

 D (2) = Disagree. You disagree more than you agree with the statement as it applies to this course or instructor.

SD (1) = Strongly Disagree. You strongly disagree with the statement as it applies to this course or instructor.

	NA	SA	A	D	SD
1. The instructor's objectives for the course have been made clear	0	4	3	2	1
2. There was considerable agreement between the announced objectives of the course and what was actually taught	0	4	3	2	1
3. The instructor used class time well	0	4	3	2	1
4. The instructor was readily available for consultation with students	0	4	3	2	1
5. The instructor seemed to know when students didn't understand the material	0	4	3	2	1
6. Lectures were too repetitive of what was in the textbook(s)	0	4	3	2	1
7. The instructor encouraged students to think for themselves	0	4	3	2	1
8. The instructor seemed genuinely concerned with students' progress and was actively helpful	0	4	3	2	1
9. The instructor made helpful comments on papers or exams	0	4	3	2	1
10. The instructor raised challenging questions or problems for discussion	0	4	3	2	1
11. In this class I felt free to ask questions or express my opinions	0	4	3	2	1
12. The instructor was well prepared for each class	0	4	3	2	1
13. The instructor told students how they would be evaluated in the course	0	4	3	2	1
14. The instructor summarized or emphasized major points in lectures or discussions	0	4	3	2	1
15. My interest in the subject area has been stimulated by this course	0	4	3	2	1
16. The scope of the course has been too limited; not enough material has been covered	0	4	3	2	1
17. Examinations reflected the important aspects of the course	0	4	3	2	1
18. I have been putting a good deal of effort into this course	0	4	3	2	1
19. The instructor was open to other viewpoints	0	4	3	2	1
20. In my opinion, the instructor has accomplished (is accomplishing) his or her objectives for the course	0	4	3	2	1

SECTION II. Items 21-31. Blacken one response number for each question.

21. For my preparation and ability, the level of difficulty of this course was:

1 Very elementary   4 Somewhat difficult
2 Somewhat elementary   5 Very difficult
3 About right

22. The work load for this course in relation to other courses of equal credit was:

1 Much lighter   4 Heavier
2 Lighter   5 Much heavier
3 About the same

23. For me, the pace at which the instructor covered the material during the term was:

1 Very slow   4 Somewhat fast
2 Somewhat slow   5 Very fast
3 Just about right

24. To what extent did the instructor use examples or illustrations to help clarify the material?

4 Frequently   2 Seldom
3 Occasionally   1 Never

Questionnaire continued on the other side

ETS 1631

Reproduced with permission

APPENDIX A (Continued)

25. Was class size satisfactory for the method of conducting the class?
- ① Yes, most of the time
- ② No, class was too large
- ③ No, class was too small
- ④ It didn't make any difference one way or the other

26. Which one of the following best describes this course for you?
- ① Major requirement or elective within major field
- ② Minor requirement or required elective outside major field
- ③ College requirement but not part of my major or minor field
- ④ Elective not required in any way
- ⑤ Other

27. Which one of the following was your most important reason for selecting this course?
- ① Friend(s) recommended it
- ② Faculty advisor's recommendation
- ③ Teacher's excellent reputation
- ④ Thought I could make a good grade
- ⑤ Could use pass/no credit option
- ⑥ It was required
- ⑦ Subject was of interest
- ⑧ Other

28. What grade do you expect to receive in this course?
- ① A
- ② B
- ③ C
- ④ D
- ⑤ Fail
- ⑥ Pass
- ⑦ No credit
- ⑧ Other

29. What is your approximate cumulative grade-point average?
- ① 3.50–4.00
- ② 3.00–3.49
- ③ 2.50–2.99
- ④ 2.00–2.49
- ⑤ 1.50–1.99
- ⑥ 1.00–1.49
- ⑦ Less than 1.00
- ⑧ None yet – first year or transfer

30. What is your class level?
- ① Freshman
- ② Sophomore
- ③ Junior
- ④ Senior
- ⑤ Graduate
- ⑥ Other

31. Sex:
- ① Female
- ② Male

SECTION III. Items 32–39. Blacken one response number for each question.

	Not applicable, don't know, or there were none	Excellent	Good	Satisfactory	Fair	Poor
32. Overall, I would rate the textbook(s)	⓪	⑤	④	③	②	①
33. Overall, I would rate the supplementary readings	⓪	⑤	④	③	②	①
34. Overall, I would rate the quality of the exams	⓪	⑤	④	③	②	①
35. I would rate the general quality of the lectures	⓪	⑤	④	③	②	①
36. I would rate the overall value of class discussions	⓪	⑤	④	③	②	①
37. Overall, I would rate the laboratories	⓪	⑤	④	③	②	①
38. I would rate the overall value of this course to me as	⓪	⑤	④	③	②	①

39. How would you rate the quality of instruction in this course? (Try to set aside your feelings about the course itself.) Blacken one response number.

Excellent	Good	About Average	Fair	Poor
⑤	④	③	②	①

SECTION IV. Items 40–49. If the instructor provided supplementary questions and response options, use this section for responding. Blacken only one response number for each question.

	NA		NA		NA	
40.	⓪	①②③④⑤⑥⑦⑧⑨	44. ⓪	①②③④⑤⑥⑦⑧⑨	48. ⓪	①②③④⑤⑥⑦⑧⑨
41.	⓪	①②③④⑤⑥⑦⑧⑨	45. ⓪	①②③④⑤⑥⑦⑧⑨	49. ⓪	①②③④⑤⑥⑦⑧⑨
42.	⓪	①②③④⑤⑥⑦⑧⑨	46. ⓪	①②③④⑤⑥⑦⑧⑨		
43.	⓪	①②③④⑤⑥⑦⑧⑨	47. ⓪	①②③④⑤⑥⑦⑧⑨		

If you would like to make additional comments about the course or instruction, use a separate sheet of paper. You might elaborate on the particular aspects you liked most as well as those you liked least. Also, how can the course or the way it was taught be improved? PLEASE GIVE THESE COMMENTS TO THE INSTRUCTOR.

If you have any comments, suggestions, or complaints about this questionnaire (for example, the content or responses available), please send them to: Student Instructional Report, Educational Testing Service, Princeton, New Jersey 08541.

This form can be processed only on an NCS Transoptic Scanner.

APPENDIX B School of Education, University of Virginia Course Evaluation Form

This questionnaire provides you with the opportunity to evaluate this course and the instructor. Your responses will be totally anonymous. The results will be used to provide a basis for course improvement and overall assessment of the effectiveness of the course.

SECTION I. *Items 1 through 25 should be answered according to the following scale: Strongly Agree (SA), Agree (A), Disagree (D), Strongly Disagree (SD), or Not Applicable or Do Not Know (NA).* **ANSWER ON TEST ANSWER SHEET PROVIDED.**

		SA	A	D	SD	NA
1.	The objectives (goals, purposes) of this course were made clear.	A	B	C	D	E
2.	The content of this course was organized and structured in a meaningful way.	A	B	C	D	E
3.	Class sessions were intellectually stimulating.	A	B	C	D	E
4.	Assignments in this course were clear and challenging.	A	B	C	D	E
5.	Teaching methods were flexible enough to accommodate individual differences.	A	B	C	D	E
6.	I am aware of how I would be evaluated in this course.	A	B	C	D	E
7.	Evaluation and grading of my work was fair and impartial.	A	B	C	D	E
8.	The instructor was well prepared for each class session.	A	B	C	D	E
9.	The instructor made clear presentations.	A	B	C	D	E
10.	The instructor was responsive to student questions and interests.	A	B	C	D	E
11.	The instructor was open to points of view other than his or her own.	A	B	C	D	E
12.	The instructor was accessible for conferences out-of-class.	A	B	C	D	E
13.	The level of difficulty in this course was suitable for my background and ability.	A	B	C	D	E
14.	The amount of work required in this course was about right.	A	B	C	D	E
15.	I spent a great deal of effort in this course.	A	B	C	D	E
16.	The objectives (goals, purposes) in this course were met.	A	B	C	D	E
17.	My interest in this subject has increased.	A	B	C	D	E
18.	I learned a great deal in this course.	A	B	C	D	E
19.	Overall, this course was worthwhile to me.	A	B	C	D	E
20.	Overall, the instructor in this course was effective.	A	B	C	D	E

Your instructor *may* furnish additional items for you to assess. Otherwise, skip to SECTION II.

21. _____

   _____   A   B   C   D   E

APPENDIX B Continued

	SA	A	D	SD	NA
22. _____					
_____	A	B	C	D	E
23. _____					
_____	A	B	C	D	E
24. _____					
_____	A	B	C	D	E
25. _____					
_____	A	B	C	D	E

SECTION II. *Below are some items about yourself that will help us to improve this questionnaire and use the results more effectively. Circle the appropriate letter.*

26. Are you an:
  A   undergraduate student
  B   graduate student in master's program
  C   graduate student in doctoral program
  D   professional development student
  E   other

27. When registering for this course, how strongly did you want to take it?
  A   very enthusiastic about it
  B   enthusiastic
  C   indifferent
  D   unenthusiastic
  E   not at all interested in taking this course

28. Which *one* of the following was the most important reason for enrolling in this course?
  A   the course is required
  B   the course is optional, but recommended
  C   the subject was of interest to me
  D   the instructor's excellent reputation
  E   I thought I could make a good grade

29. What grade do you expect in this course?
  A   A+, A, A-
  B   B+, B, B-
  C   C+, C, C-
  D   less than a C- or U
  E   other (IN, p, s, etc.)

30. Compared to other students in this course, how would you rate your own ability?
  A   well above average (top 20%)
  B   above average (next 20%)
  C   average (middle 20%)
  D   below average (next 20%)
  E   well below average (bottom 20%)

31. How many credits are you carrying this term?
  A   more than 16
  B   13-16
  C   9-12
  D   5-8
  E   0-4

APPENDIX B Continued

COURSE SCHEDULE NO. _____

SECTION III. Strengths and Weaknesses
Please make an assessment of the following specific course features by checking whether each feature was a "strong" aspect, a "neutral" aspect or a "weak" aspect of the course. Mark "not applicable" (NA) if the course did not include the particular feature. **PLACE ANSWERS ON THIS FORM.**

	Strong	Neutral	Weak	NA
lectures	( )	( )	( )	( )
discussions	( )	( )	( )	( )
textbooks	( )	( )	( )	( )
supplementary readings	( )	( )	( )	( )
labs	( )	( )	( )	( )
practica/field work	( )	( )	( )	( )
projects	( )	( )	( )	( )
term paper	( )	( )	( )	( )
exams	( )	( )	( )	( )
syllabus/reading list	( )	( )	( )	( )
audio-visual aids	( )	( )	( )	( )
tutorials	( )	( )	( )	( )
resource persons	( )	( )	( )	( )
student participation	( )	( )	( )	( )
_____	( )	( )	( )	( )
_____	( )	( )	( )	( )

OPEN REMARKS/SUGGESTIONS. *Indicate below any other remarks, assessments and/or suggestions you may have.*

APPENDIX C USC Course/Instructor Evaluation Form

USC EVALUATION SERVICES

AS A DESCRIPTION OF THIS COURSE/INSTRUCTOR, THIS STATEMENT IS:
SELECT THE BEST RESPONSE FOR EACH OF THE FOLLOWING STATEMENTS, LEAVING A RESPONSE BLANK ONLY IF IT IS CLEARLY NOT RELEVANT

(Left margin, vertical text): PUT INSTRUCTOR'S NAME & COMMENTS ON BACK—USE PENCIL ONLY, NOT PEN—COMPLETELY ERASE ANY RESPONSES YOU CHANGE

Response scale: VERY POOR (1), POOR (2), FAIR (3), GOOD (4), VERY GOOD (5)

#	Statement	1	2	3	4	5
1 LEARNING:	YOU FOUND THE COURSE INTELLECTUALLY CHALLENGING AND STIMULATING	1	2	3	4	5
2	YOU HAVE LEARNED SOMETHING WHICH YOU CONSIDER VALUABLE	1	2	3	4	5
3	YOUR INTEREST IN THE SUBJECT HAS INCREASED AS A CONSEQUENCE OF THIS COURSE	1	2	3	4	5
4	YOU HAVE LEARNED AND UNDERSTOOD THE SUBJECT MATERIALS IN THIS COURSE	1	2	3	4	5
5 ENTHUSIASM:	INSTRUCTOR WAS ENTHUSIASTIC ABOUT TEACHING THE COURSE	1	2	3	4	5
6	INSTRUCTOR WAS DYNAMIC AND ENERGETIC IN CONDUCTING THE COURSE	1	2	3	4	5
7	INSTRUCTOR ENHANCED PRESENTATIONS WITH THE USE OF HUMOR	1	2	3	4	5
8	INSTRUCTOR'S STYLE OF PRESENTATION HELD YOUR INTEREST DURING CLASS	1	2	3	4	5
9 ORGANIZATION:	INSTRUCTOR'S EXPLANATIONS WERE CLEAR	1	2	3	4	5
10	COURSE MATERIALS WERE WELL PREPARED AND CAREFULLY EXPLAINED	1	2	3	4	5
11	PROPOSED OBJECTIVES AGREED WITH THOSE ACTUALLY TAUGHT SO YOU KNEW WHERE COURSE WAS GOING	1	2	3	4	5
12	INSTRUCTOR GAVE LECTURES THAT FACILITATED TAKING NOTES	1	2	3	4	5
13 GROUP INTERACTION:	STUDENTS WERE ENCOURAGED TO PARTICIPATE IN CLASS DISCUSSIONS	1	2	3	4	5
14	STUDENTS WERE INVITED TO SHARE THEIR IDEAS AND KNOWLEDGE	1	2	3	4	5
15	STUDENTS WERE ENCOURAGED TO ASK QUESTIONS & WERE GIVEN MEANINGFUL ANSWERS	1	2	3	4	5
16	STUDENTS WERE ENCOURAGED TO EXPRESS THEIR OWN IDEAS AND/OR QUESTION THE INSTRUCTOR	1	2	3	4	5
17 INDIVIDUAL RAPPORT:	INSTRUCTOR WAS FRIENDLY TOWARDS INDIVIDUAL STUDENTS	1	2	3	4	5
18	INSTRUCTOR MADE STUDENTS FEEL WELCOME IN SEEKING HELP/ADVICE IN OR OUTSIDE OF CLASS	1	2	3	4	5
19	INSTRUCTOR HAD A GENUINE INTEREST IN INDIVIDUAL STUDENTS	1	2	3	4	5
20	INSTRUCTOR WAS ADEQUATELY ACCESSIBLE TO STUDENTS DURING OFFICE HOURS OR AFTER CLASS	1	2	3	4	5
21 BREADTH:	INSTRUCTOR CONTRASTED THE IMPLICATIONS OF VARIOUS THEORIES	1	2	3	4	5
22	INSTRUCTOR PRESENTED THE BACKGROUND OR ORIGIN OF IDEAS/CONCEPTS DEVELOPED IN CLASS	1	2	3	4	5
23	INSTRUCTOR PRESENTED POINTS OF VIEW OTHER THAN HIS/HER OWN WHEN APPROPRIATE	1	2	3	4	5
24	INSTRUCTOR ADEQUATELY DISCUSSED CURRENT DEVELOPMENTS IN THE FIELD	1	2	3	4	5
25 EXAMINATIONS:	FEEDBACK ON EXAMINATIONS/GRADED MATERIALS WAS VALUABLE	1	2	3	4	5
26	METHODS OF EVALUATING STUDENT WORK WERE FAIR AND APPROPRIATE	1	2	3	4	5
27	EXAMINATIONS/GRADED MATERIALS TESTED COURSE CONTENT AS EMPHASIZED BY THE INSTRUCTOR	1	2	3	4	5
28 ASSIGNMENTS:	REQUIRED READINGS/TEXTS WERE VALUABLE	1	2	3	4	5
29	READINGS, HOMEWORK, ETC. CONTRIBUTED TO APPRECIATION AND UNDERSTANDING OF SUBJECT	1	2	3	4	5
30 OVERALL:	HOW DOES THIS COURSE COMPARE WITH OTHER COURSES YOU HAVE HAD AT USC?	1	2	3	4	5
31	HOW DOES THIS INSTRUCTOR COMPARE WITH OTHER INSTRUCTORS YOU HAVE HAD AT USC?	1	2	3	4	5

STUDENT AND COURSE CHARACTERISTICS (LEAVE BLANK IF NO RESPONSE APPLIES)

#	Statement	1	2	3	4	5
32	COURSE DIFFICULTY, RELATIVE TO OTHER COURSES, WAS (1-VERY EASY... 3-MEDIUM ... 5-VERY HARD)	1	2	3	4	5
33	COURSE WORKLOAD, RELATIVE TO OTHER COURSES, WAS (1-VERY LIGHT.. 3-MEDIUM 5-VERY HEAVY)	1	2	3	4	5
34	COURSE PACE WAS (1-TOO SLOW... 3-ABOUT RIGHT... 5-TOO FAST)	1	2	3	4	5
35	HOURS WEEK REQUIRED OUTSIDE OF CLASS 1 0 TO 2 2 2 TO 5 3 5 TO 7 4 8 TO 12 5 OVER 12	1	2	3	4	5
36	LEVEL OF INTEREST IN THE SUBJECT PRIOR TO THIS COURSE (1-VERY LOW... 3-MEDIUM ... 5-VERY HIGH)	1	2	3	4	5
37	OVERALL GPA AT USC 1 BELOW 2.5 2 2.5 TO 3.0 3 3.0 TO 3.4 4 3.4 TO 3.7 5 ABOVE 3.7 LEAVE BLANK IF NOT YET ESTABLISHED AT USC	1	2	3	4	5
38	EXPECTED GRADE IN THE COURSE (1-F, 2-D, 3-C, 4-B, 5-A)	F	D	C	B	A
39	REASON FOR TAKING THE COURSE 1 MAJOR REQUIRE 2 MAJOR ELECTIVE 3 GENERAL ED REQUIRE 4-MINOR RELATED FIELD 5 GENERAL INTEREST ONLY SELECT THE ONE WHICH IS BEST	1	2	3	4	5
40	YEAR IN SCHOOL 1) FRESH. 2) SOPH. 3) JR. 4) SR. 5) GRAD.	1	2	3	4	5
41	MAJOR DEPARTMENT 1 SOC SCI/COMM 2 NAT SCI/MATH 3 HUMANITIES 4 BUSINESS 5 EDUCATION	1	2	3	4	5
	6 ENGINEERING 7 PERF ARTS 8 PUB AFFAIRS 9/OTHER 10 UNDECLARED/UNDECIDED	6	7	8	9	10

SUPPLEMENTAL QUESTIONS (USE RESPONSES BELOW FOR INSTRUCTOR'S QUESTIONS)

#						#						#				
42	1	2	3	4	5	47	1	2	3	4	5	52	1	2	3	4	5	57	1	2	3	4	5
43	1	2	3	4	5	48	1	2	3	4	5	53	1	2	3	4	5	58	1	2	3	4	5
44	1	2	3	4	5	49	1	2	3	4	5	54	1	2	3	4	5	59	1	2	3	4	5
45	1	2	3	4	5	50	1	2	3	4	5	55	1	2	3	4	5	60	1	2	3	4	5
46	1	2	3	4	5	51	1	2	3	4	5	56	1	2	3	4	5	61	1	2	3	4	5

APPENDIX C (Continued)

INSTRUCTOR'S NAME	DEPARTMENT NAME	COURSE NUMBER

INSTRUCTIONS

This evaluation form is intended to measure your reactions to this instructor and course. Results will be reported to the Department Chairmen to be used as part of the overall evaluation of the instructor. These evaluations will have budgetary and promotional implications so please take it very seriously. When you have finished a designated student will pick up the evaluations and take them to the Department Chairperson. Your responses will remain anonymous and summaries will not be given to the instructor until after the final grades have been assigned.

****Put Instructor's Name, Department Name and Course Number at top
(i.e., Smith, Psychology, 200)
****Use a number 2 pencil, do not use ink, ball point, magic marker, etc
****Blacken only one response for each question and erase any changes completely

OPEN-ENDED COMMENTS

PLEASE INDICATE THE IMPORTANT CHARACTERISTICS OF THIS INSTRUCTOR/COURSE WHICH HAVE BEEN MOST VALUABLE TO YOUR LEARNING EXPERIENCE.

1.
2.
3.

PLEASE INDICATE CHARACTERISTICS OF THIS INSTRUCTOR/COURSE WHICH YOU FEEL ARE MOST IMPORTANT FOR HIM/HER TO WORK ON IMPROVING (PARTICULARLY ASPECTS NOT COVERED ABOVE).

1.
2.
3.

PLEASE USE THE ADDITIONAL SPACE TO CLARIFY ANY OF YOUR RESPONSES OR TO MAKE OTHER COMMENTS.

APPENDIX D   IDEA Survey Form—Student Reactions to Instruction and Courses

Your thoughtful answers to these questions will provide helpful information to your instructor.

> • Describe the frequency of your instructor's teaching procedures, using the following code:
> 1—Hardly Ever   3—Sometimes
> 2—Occasionally   4—Frequently   5—Almost Always

The Instructor:

1. Promoted teacher-student discussion (as opposed to mere responses to questions).
2. Found ways to help students answer their own questions.
3. Encouraged students to express themselves freely and openly.
4. Seemed enthusiastic about the subject matter.
5. Changed approaches to meet new situations.
6. Gave examinations which stressed unnecessary memorization.
7. Spoke with expressiveness and variety in tone of voice.
8. Demonstrated the importance and significance of the subject matter.
9. Made presentations which were dry and dull.
10. Made it clear how each topic fit into the course.
11. Explained the reasons for criticisms of students' academic performance.
12. Gave examination questions which were unclear.
13. Encouraged student comments even when they turned out to be incorrect or irrelevant.
14. Summarized material in a manner which aided retention.
15. Stimulated students to intellectual effort beyond that required by most courses.
16. Clearly stated the objectives of the course.
17. Explained course material clearly, and explanations were to the point.
18. Related course material to real life situations.
19. Gave examination questions which were unreasonably detailed (picky).
20. Introduced stimulating ideas about the subject.

> • On each of the objectives listed below, rate the progress you have made in this course compared with that made in other courses you have taken at this college or university. In this course my progress was:
> 1—Low (lowest 10 percent of courses I have taken here)
> 2—Low Average (next 20 percent of courses)
> 3—Average (middle 40 percent of courses)
> 4—High Average (next 20 percent of courses)
> 5—High (highest 10 percent of courses)

Progress on:

21. Gaining factual knowledge (terminology, classifications, methods, trends).
22. Learning fundamental principles, generalizations, or theories.
23. Learning to apply course material to improve rational thinking, problem-solving and decision-making.
24. Developing specific skills, competencies and points of view needed by professionals in the field most closely related to this course.
25. Learning how professionals in this field go about the process of gaining new knowledge.
26. Developing creative capacities.
27. Developing a sense of personal responsibility (self-reliance, self-discipline).
28. Gaining a broader understanding and appreciation of intellectual-cultural activity (music, science, literature, etc.).
29. Developing skill in expressing myself orally or in writing.
30. Discovering the implications of the course material for understanding myself (interests, talents, values, etc.).

> • On the next four questions, compare this course with others you have taken at this institution, using the following code:
> 1—Much Less than Most Courses
> 2—Less than Most
> 3—About Average
> 4—More than Most
> 5—Much More than Most

The Course:

31. Amount of reading.
32. Amount of work in other (non-reading) assignments.
33. Difficulty of subject matter.
34. Degree to which the course hung together (various topics and class activities were related to each other).

> • Describe your attitudes toward and behavior in this course, using the following code:
> 1—Definitely False
> 2—More False than True   4—More True than False
> 3—In Between   5—Definitely True

Self-rating:

35. I worked harder on this course than on most courses I have taken.
36. I had a strong desire to take this course.
37. I would like to take another course from this instructor.
38. As a result of taking this course, I have more positive feelings toward this field of study.
39. Leave this space blank. Continue with question A.

A. Blacken space number 5 on the Response Card.

> • For the following six questions, B-G, indicate how well each of the following statements describes the students in this class by blackening the proper space.
> 1—Definitely False
> 2—More False than True   4—More True than False
> 3—In Between   5—Definitely True

B. The students in this class are angry about grades.
C. The students in this class use their mistakes as opportunities to learn.
D. The students in this class take responsibility for their own learning.
E. The students in this class think they are wasting their time.
F. The students in this class are bored.
G. The students in this class have interesting and useful discussions.

If your instructor has extra questions, answer them in the space designated on the Response Card.

Your comments are invited on how the instructor might improve this course or teaching procedures. Use the back of the Response Card (unless otherwise directed).

APPENDIX E ICES Instructor and Course Evaluation Form

SIDE 1   **INSTRUCTOR AND COURSE EVALUATION SYSTEM**

SPECIAL INSTRUCTIONS

SPECIAL CODE   **For:**

ABCDE   ECON FACULTY   ECON 396 A   SU 83
See Side 2 for directions. Use pencil only on this side.

1. When registering, what was your opinion about the	2. Course in	3. Sex	
	○ Major	○ Male	00—
	○ Minor	○ Female	1
	○ Other	5 Class	6 Expected Grade
4 This course was	○ Fresh	○ Ⓐ
○ Specifically required	○ Soph	Ⓑ
○ Required but a choice among several	○ Junior	Ⓒ
Instructor	○ Senior	Ⓓ
Course	○ An elective	○ Grad / ○ Other	Ⓕ

Special Instructions:
A) For Items ...... Respond
I, J, K, L, M
B) For Items ...... Respond
I, J, K, L, M

1. RATE THE COURSE CONTENT	EXCELLENT ○○○○○○ VERY POOR
2. RATE THE INSTRUCTOR	EXCELLENT ○○○○○○ VERY POOR
3. RATE THE COURSE IN GENERAL	EXCELLENT ○○○○○○ VERY POOR
4. THE INSTRUCTOR WAS CONSCIENTIOUS ABOUT HIS/HER INSTRUCTIONAL RESPONSIBILITIES.	STRONGLY AGREE ⒤Ⓙ Ⓚ Ⓛ Ⓜ STRONGLY DISAGREE
5. THE GRADING PROCEDURES FOR THE COURSE WERE:	VERY FAIR ⒤Ⓙ Ⓚ Ⓛ Ⓜ VERY UNFAIR
6. HOW WELL DID EXAMINATION QUESTIONS RE-FLECT CONTENT AND EMPHASIS OF THE COURSE?	WELL RELATED ⒤Ⓙ Ⓚ Ⓛ Ⓜ POORLY RELATED
7. WAS THE PROGRESSION OF THE COURSE LOGI-CAL AND COHERENT FROM BEGINNING TO END?	YES, ALWAYS ⒤Ⓙ Ⓚ Ⓛ Ⓜ NO, SELDOM
8. HOW WOULD YOU CHARACTERIZE THE INSTRUC-TOR'S ABILITY TO EXPLAIN?	EXCELLENT ⒤Ⓙ Ⓚ Ⓛ Ⓜ VERY POOR
9. THE INSTRUCTOR MOTIVATED ME TO DO MY BEST WORK.	ALMOST ALWAYS ⒤Ⓙ Ⓚ Ⓛ Ⓜ ALMOST NEVER
10. DID THIS COURSE INCREASE YOUR INTEREST IN THE SUBJECT MATTER?	YES, GREATLY ⒤Ⓙ Ⓚ Ⓛ Ⓜ NO, NOT MUCH
11. DID THIS COURSE IMPROVE YOUR UNDERSTANDING OF CONCEPTS AND PRINCIPLES IN THIS FIELD?	YES, SIG-NIFICANTLY ⒤Ⓙ Ⓚ Ⓛ Ⓜ NO, NOT MUCH
12. THE COURSE CONTENT WAS:	TOO THEORETICAL ⒤Ⓙ Ⓚ Ⓛ Ⓜ TOO APPLIED
13. DID THE INSTRUCTOR PRESENT MATERIAL THAT WAS NOT COVERED IN OUTSIDE READINGS?	YES, OFTEN ⒤Ⓙ Ⓚ Ⓛ Ⓜ NO, SELDOM
14. THE INSTRUCTOR DEFINED THE OBJECTIVES OF DISCUSSION.	ALMOST ALW-AYS OCCURED ⒤Ⓙ Ⓚ Ⓛ Ⓜ ALMOST NEV-ER OCCURRED
15. WERE WRITTEN ASSIGNMENTS GRADED FAIRLY?	YES, QUITE FAIR ⒤Ⓙ Ⓚ Ⓛ Ⓜ NO, VERY UNFAIR
16. WERE REQUESTS FOR RE-GRADING OR REVIEW HANDLED FAIRLY?	YES, ALMOST ALWAYS ⒤Ⓙ Ⓚ Ⓛ Ⓜ NO, ALMOST NEVER
17	⒤Ⓙ Ⓚ Ⓛ Ⓜ
18.	⒤Ⓙ Ⓚ Ⓛ Ⓜ
19	⒤Ⓙ Ⓚ Ⓛ Ⓜ
20	⒤Ⓙ Ⓚ Ⓛ Ⓜ
21	⒤Ⓙ Ⓚ Ⓛ Ⓜ
22	⒤Ⓙ Ⓚ Ⓛ Ⓜ
23	⒤Ⓙ Ⓚ Ⓛ Ⓜ
24	⒤Ⓙ Ⓚ Ⓛ Ⓜ
25	⒤Ⓙ Ⓚ Ⓛ Ⓜ
26	⒤Ⓙ Ⓚ Ⓛ Ⓜ

APPENDIX E (Continued)

DIRECTIONS FOR ICES   SIDE 2

Please use this side of the form for your personal comments on teacher effectiveness and other aspects of the course.   Use pencil only in responding to the objective questions on the reverse side.
Objective items 1-3 will be used to compare this course and instructor to others in the department and institution   Data from other items after item 3 would be useful to the instructor for course improvements. Your instructor will not see your completed evaluation until final grades are in for your course

NOTE:
Someone other than your instructor should collect and mail these forms.

DO NOT WRITE IN THE SHADED AREA

PLEASE WRITE COMMENTS BELOW

A What are the major strengths and weaknesses of the instructor?

B What aspects of this course were most beneficial to you?

C What do you suggest to improve this course?

D Comment on the grading procedures and exams.

E Instructor option question

F Instructor option question

APPENDIX F Sample ICES Instructor Report

FOR: D. Johnson   DEPT ECON   COURSE 302   SECTION C   DEPT CODE 17200   SEMESTER: Spring YEAR 1983

DEMOGRAPHIC DATA IN PERCENTS
NO. OF FORMS COMPLETED: 34

1. PRE-COURSE OPINION TOWARD

	POS	NO OP	NEG	OMIT
INSTRUCTOR	38	62	0	0
COURSE	76	21	0	3

4. THIS COURSE WAS:

SPECIFICALLY REQUIRED	REQUIRED BUT A CHOICE	ELECTIVE	OMIT
0	71	29	0

2. COURSE IN:

MAJOR	MINOR	OTHER	OMIT
35	3	62	0

5. CLASS STATUS:

FRESH	SOPH	JUNIOR	SENIOR	GRAD	OTHER	OMIT
0	3	44	53	0	0	0

3. SEX:

MALE	FEMALE	OMIT
6	88	6

6. EXPECTED GRADE:

A	B	C	D	E	OMIT	*EXP GRADE MEAN*
44	47	6	0	0	3	4.4

GLOBAL CORE ITEM RESULTS

		RESPONSE LABELS, PERCENTS & FREQUENCIES( )					SUMMARY STATISTICS			*RELATIVE COMPARISON OF CLASS MEAN GROUP 1: MIXED REQ/FACULTY GROUP 2: ECONOMICS FACULTY			
ITEM	WEIGHTS	--5--	--4--	3	--2--	OMIT	MEAN	SD			LOW	AVG	HIGH
		EXCELLENT			VERY POOR		MDN	CONS		LOW	AVG	AVG	HI
1 RATE THE COURSE CONTENT		35 36(12)	26 13(16)	9 0(0)	0 0(0)	0 0(0)	5.1 5.1	0.76 2		1		DOOXOO	OOOXOO
2 RATE THE INSTRUCTOR		47 47(16)	38 13(13)	6 0(0)	0 0(0)	0 0(0)	5.3 5.4	0.84 1 2			OOOXOO	OOOXOO	
3 RATE THE COURSE IN GENERAL		26 9(9)	47 61(21)	18 21(0)	0 0(0)	0 0(0)	5.0 5.0	0.83 1 2			DOXOO	OOOXOO	

INTERPRETATION GUIDE

THE UPPER PORTION OF THIS PAGE OF THE COMPUTER PRINTOUT CONTAINS PERCENTAGES OF STUDENTS WHO MARKED EACH RESPONSE OPTION FOR THE DEMOGRAPHIC ITEMS. FOR DEMOGRAPHIC #6 THE EXPECTED GRADE MEAN IS CALCULATED USING A WEIGHT OF 5 FOR A, ETC. GLOBAL ITEM RESULTS (ITEM 1, 2, AND 3) ARE PRESENTED NEXT. THE TOP ROWS CONTAIN PERCENTAGES; BOTTOM ROWS CONTAIN NUMBERS OF STUDENTS MARKING EACH OPTION. LABELS, PERCENTS AND FREQUENCIES FOR EACH ROW ARE INDICATED ABOVE EACH RESPONSE OPTION. FOR GLOBAL ITEMS THE RANGE IS 1-6 WITH 6 THE SUMMARY STATISTICS ARE CALCULATED USING WEIGHTS INDICATED USING MEAN. THE RANGE IS 1-5 WITH 5 MOST FAVORABLE. MOST FAVORABLE FOR MOST OTHER ITEMS THE RANGE IS 1-5 WITH 5 MOST FAVORABLE. CONS (CONSENSUS): POSSIBLE VALUES ARE HIGH, AVG OR LOW. HIGH INDICATES CONSIDERABLE STUDENT AGREEMENT.

RELATIVE COMPARISON: CLASS MEAN RATING IS COMPARED WITH ONE OR TWO GROUPS. GROUP 1 IS CAMPUS-WIDE BASED ON REQUIRED/ELECTIVE NATURE OF COURSE AND INSTRUCTOR RANK. GROUP 2 IS DEPARTMENT-WIDE. THE RELATIVE POSITION OF THE CLASS MEAN IS DENOTED UNDER ONE OF THE FOLLOWING FIVE NORM CATEGORIES.

HI--TOP 10%; HIGH AVG--NEXT 20%; AVG--MIDDLE 40%; LOW AVG--NEXT 20%; OR LOW--BOTTOM 10%

THE ROWS CONTAINING AN X AND O'S SHOW THE CLASS AVERAGE RATING IN COMPARISON TO GROUPS 1 AND 2. X INDICATES THE RELATIVE PLACEMENT OF THE MEAN. O'S INDICATE THE RANGE OF UNCERTAINTY. THE RATINGS SHOULD BE READ, FOR EXAMPLE, AS LOW-AVERAGE TO AVERAGE OR HIGH-AVERAGE TO HIGH TO TAKE INTO ACCOUNT THE RANGE OF UNCERTAINTY.

STUDENT RESPONSES TO DEPARTMENTAL CORE ITEMS, INSTRUCTOR SELECTED ITEMS OR COMPLETE FORM ITEMS ARE PRESENTED NEXT. THE RESULTS ARE TO BE INTERPRETED IN THE SAME WAY. HOWEVER, NORMATIVE DATA MAY NOT BE AVAILABLE.

98

INSTRUCTOR AND COURSE EVALUATION SYSTEM   INSTRUCTOR REPORT D. Johnson   ECON 302 C   17200   NO. FORMS   34   SP 83   PAGE 2

DEPARTMENTAL CORE ITEM RESULTS

RESPONSE LABELS, PERCENTS & FREQUENCIES | SUMMARY STATISTICS | RELATIVE COMPARISON OF CLASS MEAN

4 THE INSTRUCTOR WAS CONSCIENTIOUS ABOUT HIS/HER INSTRUCTIONAL RESPONSIBILITIES.
CATALOG ITEM 278
WEIGHTING SCHEME 54321

STRONGLY AGREE			STRONGLY DISAGREE	OMIT	MEAN MDN	SD CONS
68 (23)	26 (9)	6 (2)	0 (0)	0 (0)	4.6 / 4.6	0.59 AVG

ECONOMICS FACULTY
LOW ! AVG ! HI : LOW! AVG! AVG !AVG!HI
OOXOOO

5 THE GRADING PROCEDURES FOR THE COURSE WERE:
CATALOG ITEM 101
WEIGHTING SCHEME 54321

VERY FAIR			VERY UNFAIR	OMIT	MEAN MDN	SD CONS
12 (4)	29 (10)	29 / 21	9 (3)	0 (0)	3.1 / 3.2	1.14 LOW

LOW ! HI : LOW! AVG! AVG !AVG!HI
#XOO

6 HOW WELL DID EXAMINATION QUESTIONS REFLECT CONTENT AND EMPHASIS OF THE COURSE?
CATALOG ITEM 103
WEIGHTING SCHEME 54321

WELL RELATED			POORLY RELATED	OMIT	MEAN MDN	SD CONS
15 (5)	41 (14)	29 (10)	9 (3)	6 (2)	3.5 / 3.6	1.03 AVG

LOW ! HI : LOW! AVG! AVG !AVG!HI
OOXOOO

7 WAS THE PROGRESSION OF THE COURSE LOGICAL AND COHERENT FROM BEGINNING TO END?
CATALOG ITEM 5
WEIGHTING SCHEME 54321

YES, ALWAYS			NO, SELDOM	OMIT	MEAN MDN	SD CONS
38	50	9	3	0	4.2 / 4.2	0.73

LOW ! HI : LOW! AVG! AVG !AVG!HI

. . .   .

INSTRUCTOR SELECTED ITEMS RESULTS

MESSAGES

14 THE INSTRUCTOR CHANGED APPROACHES WHEN THE OCCASION DEMANDED IT.
CATALOG ITEM 25
WEIGHTING SCHEME 54321

STRONGLY AGREE			STRONGLY DISAGREE	OMIT	MEAN MDN	SD
70 (19)	26 (7)	4 (1)	0 (0)	0 (0)	4.7 / 4.6	0.54

MEAN-PROBABLE STRENGTH
SD SHOWS AVG AGREEMENT
HI RESPONSE WEIGHT 5

15 I NEEDED MORE DIRECTION.
CATALOG ITEM 26
WEIGHTING SCHEME 12345

STRONGLY AGREE			STRONGLY DISAGREE	OMIT	MEAN MDN	SD
7 (2)	4 (1)	22 (6)	22 (6)	44 (12)	3.9 / 4.3	1.21

MEAN IS IN AVG RANGE
SD SHOWS LOW AGREEMENT

16 THE INSTRUCTOR PROVIDED PRACTICE FOR STUDENTS TO MASTER COURSE MATERIAL.
CATALOG ITEM 48
WEIGHTING SCHEME 54321

ALMOST ALWAYS			ALMOST NEVER	OMIT	MEAN MDN	SD
74 (20)	22 (6)	4 (1)	0 (0)	0 (0)	4.7 / 4.7	0.52

MEAN-PROBABLE STRENGTH
SD SHOWS AVG AGREEMENT
HI RESPONSE WEIGHT 5

17 DID YOUR INSTRUCTOR RELATE EXERCISES TO INFORMATION GAINED ELSEWHERE?
CATALOG ITEM 61
WEIGHTING SCHEME 54321

ALMOST ALWAYS			ALMOST NEVER	OMIT	MEAN MDN	SD
52 (14)	33 (9)	11 (3)	0 (0)	0 (0)	1	4.4 / 4.5	0.69

MEAN IS IN AVG RANGE
SD SHOWS AVG AGREEMENT

APPENDIX G

Structured Interview Schedule Outline Used at Augustana College

Procedure

1. Check to be sure that student understands the nature of "tenure."

2. Explain how the student was selected.

3. Explain how the student's opinion is not to be used as a "vote" for or against promotion.

4. Promise confidentiality.

Questions

1. Strengths and positive comments of the instructor in and out of the classroom.

2. Weaknesses and negative comments of the instructor in and out of the classroom.

3. Instructor demonstration of progress and growth. (For students enrolled in two or more of the instructor's courses.)

4. Rank the instructor with:
   (a) other faculty in the department
   (b) all college faculty

5. Should the instructor receive tenure?

6. Any additional comments.

APPENDIX H

Plan for Peer Evaluation of Teaching Activity
for the Department of Horticulture

INTRODUCTION

Peer evaluation of teaching has been proposed as a desirable input to the administrative evaluation of academic staff members. Results from student questionnaires, while useful in determining attitudes of the instructor, proficiency of presentation and to some degree knowledge of the subject, do not measure adequately such things as choice of subject matter, development of courses and laboratories, and activities outside the classroom such as writing of texts and articles and participation on teaching and courses and curricula committees.

Before peer evaluation can be organized, a definition of the word "peer" is essential. Webster's definition, "one who is on an equal standing with another," could be interpreted to include academic rank and/or technical proficiency and experience in a subject matter area. For this plan, the *technical proficiency* and *experience* will be given high priority.

Student evaluation questionnaires are equally distributed to classes each semester. It does not seem practical to obtain peer evaluation at this frequency. The staff time required would be excessive and many of the items that are appropriate for peer evaluation are not determined by the semester time frame. Consequently, peer evaluation would not be done on a regular scheduled basis but at times when it was needed or requested.

It is essential that the evaluation not be constituted as an adversary relationship between the peers and the instructor. The experience should be both evaluative and helpful and might well be at the request of the instructor whose major purpose would be improvement of the outline for his course.

THE PLAN

Peer evaluations would be made at the direction of the department head

1. for his own use in recommending promotions;

2. at his direction after approval of one of the following requests

a. from the courses and curricula committee,
b. from the instructor being evaluated,
c. at time of adding staff or changing instructors (how should course be changed or dropped).

An evaluation would be scheduled to accomplish one or more of the following:

1. to validate evidence to justify a promotion,

2. to provide assistance to an instructor for developing or improving a course,

3. to assist courses and curricula committees in evaluating course offerings,

4. to provide a systematic method of investigating significant complaints of students about course subject matter.

The Department Head in consultation with the Courses and Curriculum Committee would appoint a committee of three to conduct the evaluation. The committee would normally consist of three professors.

The instructor would assemble the following appropriate items and circulate them to the committee prior to the evaluation:

1. course outlines, daily class schedules, and reference lists (including text);

2. sample problems, examinations, laboratory reports;

3. his own written summary of his significant teaching activities including committee assignments related to teaching, development of laboratories, teaching aids, texts, articles and other teaching innovations;

4. student evaluation summaries of past semesters.

The committee would meet with the instructor and examine and discuss his teaching activities. The members of the committee would not only evaluate the instructor's performance but also make suggestions for improvement. By discussion with the instructor, the committee would rate or validate the items in the written summary of activities. To assure that each member's ideas were included in the report, the report would contain a letter from each of the three. These letters along with the instructor's written summary would then become a part of the instructor's teaching file. This evaluation would not generally include classroom visitation. Depending on the circumstances, the peer evaluation could take on several forms in addition to the basic elements listed above.

APPENDIX I

Videotape Self-Review

Suggestions for Viewing Your Videotape

A. Focus your attention on a *few* lecture skills that are of particular interest to you and that are important to student learning. Select one or more of the following rating guides to concentrate on while you view your videotape.

Rating Guides

Importance and Suitability of Content

Organization of Content

Presentation Style

Clarity of Presentation

Questioning Ability

Establishing and Maintaining Contact with Students

B. If the selected rating guide does not seem relevant to your lecturing style or subject, select another.

C. Space has been provided at the bottom of each rating guide for additional comments which come to mind as you view the tape.

D. Consider the following questions after viewing your videotape.

   1. How do your observations and data generated from the Self-Rating Guide compare with your intended goals for the lesson?

   2. Are your teaching outcomes consistent with your intent?

SOURCE: Diamond, N., Sharp, G., and Ory, J. C., *Improving Your Lecturing.* Urbana, IL: Office of Instructional Resources, University of Illinois, 1983. Used by permission.

Content: Importance and Suitability

Directions: Respond to each of the state-   1 = strength
ments below by checking the   2 = somewhat of a
number which best expresses   problem
your judgment.   3 = a major problem
4 = not applicable

		1	2	3	4
1.	The material presented is generally accepted by colleagues to be worth knowing.	—	—	—	—
2.	The material presented is important for this group of students.	—	—	—	—
3.	The instructor seemed to match the lecture material to the student's backgrounds.	—	—	—	—
4.	The examples used were easily understood by students.	—	—	—	—
5.	When appropriate, a distinction was made between factual material and opinions.	—	—	—	—
6.	Appropriate authorities were cited to support statements.	—	—	—	—
7.	When appropriate, divergent viewpoints were presented.	—	—	—	—
8.	A sufficient amount of material was included in the lecture.	—	—	—	—

Other Comments:

Content: Organization

Directions: Respond to each of the state-   1 = strength
ments below by checking the   2 = somewhat of a
number which best expresses   problem
your judgment.   3 = a major problem
      4 = not applicable

	1	2	3	4

Introduction

1. Stated the purpose of the lecture. — — — —

2. Presented a brief overview of the lecture content. — — — —

3. Stated a problem to be solved or discussed during the lecture. — — — —

4. Made explicit the relationship between today's and the previous lecture. — — — —

Body of Lecture

5. Arranged and discussed the content so that the organization/structure was made explicit to the students. — — — —

6. Asked questions periodically to determine whether too much or too little information was being presented. — — — —

7. Presented examples, illustrations or graphics to clarify abstract and difficult ideas. — — — —

8. Explicitly stated the relationships among various ideas in the lecture. — — — —

9. Periodically summarized the most important ideas in the lecture. — — — —

Conclusion

10. Solved or otherwise dealt with any problems raised during the lecture. — — — —

11. Restated what students were expected to gain from the lecture material. — — — —

12. Summarized the main ideas in the lecture. — — — —

13. Related the day's lecture to upcoming presentations. — — — —

Other Comments:

Presentation: Style

Directions: Respond to each of the statements below by checking the number which best expresses your judgment.	1 = strength 2 = somewhat of a problem 3 = a major problem 4 = not applicable

	1	2	3	4

Voice Characteristics

1. Voice could be easily heard. __ __ __ __

2. Voice was raised or lowered for variety and emphasis. __ __ __ __

3. Speech was neither too formal nor too casual. __ __ __ __

4. Speech fillers, ("okay now," "ahm,") were not distracting. __ __ __ __

5. Rate of speech was neither too fast nor too slow. __ __ __ __

Nonverbal Communication

6. Established and maintained eye contact with the class as lecture began. __ __ __ __

7. Listened carefully to student's comments and questions. __ __ __ __

8. Wasn't too stiff and formal in appearance. __ __ __ __

9. Wasn't too casual in appearance. __ __ __ __

10. Facial and body movements were consistent with instructor's intentions. For example, the instructor looked at students while waiting for their responses after asking questions. __ __ __ __

Other Comments:

Presentation: Clarity

Directions: Respond to each of the state-ments below by checking the number which best expresses your judgment.	1 = strength 2 = somewhat of a problem 3 = a major problem 4 = not applicable

	1	2	3	4
1. Stated the purpose at the beginning of the lecture.	—	—	—	—
2. Defined new terms, concepts and principles.	—	—	—	—
3. Told the students why certain processes, techniques or formulas were used to solve problems.	—	—	—	—
4. Used relevant examples to explain major ideas.	—	—	—	—
5. Used clear and simple examples.	—	—	—	—
6. Explicitly related new ideas to familiar ones.	—	—	—	—
7. Reiterated definitions of new terms to help students become accustomed to them.	—	—	—	—
8. Provided occasional summaries and restatements of important ideas.	—	—	—	—
9. Used alternate explanations when necessary.	—	—	—	—
10. Slowed the word flow when ideas were complex and difficult.	—	—	—	—
11. Did not often digress from the main topic.	—	—	—	—
12. Talked to the class, not to the board or windows.	—	—	—	—
13. The board work appeared organized and legible.	—	—	—	—

Other Comments:

Questioning Skills

Directions: Respond to each of the statements below by checking the number which best expresses your judgment.	1 = strength 2 = somewhat of a problem 3 = a major problem 4 = not applicable

	1	2	3	4
1. Asked questions to see what the students knew about the lecture topic.	—	—	—	—
2. Addressed questions to individual students as well as the group at large.	—	—	—	—
3. Used rhetorical questions to gain students' attention.	—	—	—	—
4. Paused after all questions to allow students time to think of an answer.	—	—	—	—
5. Encouraged students to answer difficult questions by providing cues or rephrasing.	—	—	—	—
6. When necessary, asked students to clarify their questions.	—	—	—	—
7. Asked probing questions if a student's answer was incomplete or superficial.	—	—	—	—
8. Repeated answers when necessary so the entire class could hear.	—	—	—	—
9. Received students' questions politely and when possible enthusiastically.	—	—	—	—
10. Requested that questions which required time-consuming answers of limited interest be discussed before or after class or during office hours.	—	—	—	—

Other Comments:

Establishing and Maintaining Contact With Students

Directions: Respond to each of the statements below by checking the
number which best expresses
your judgment.

1 = strength
2 = somewhat of a
    problem
3 = a major problem
4 = not applicable

	1	2	3	4

Establishing Contact

1. Greeted students with a bit of small talk.

2. Established eye contact with as many students as possible.

3. Set ground rules for student participation and
questioning.

4. Used questions to gain student attention.

5. Encouraged student questions.

Maintaining Contact

6. Maintained eye contact with as many students as possible.

7. Used rhetorical questions to re-engage student attention.

8. Asked questions which allowed the instructor to gauge students' progress.

9. Was able to answer students' questions satisfactorily.

10. Noted and responded to signs of puzzlement,
boredom, curiosity, etc.

11. Varied the pace of the lecture to keep students alert.

12. Spoke at a rate which allowed students time
to take notes.

Other Comments:

APPENDIX J

Evaluation of Course Materials

Listed below are several items about course materials categorized into three major areas. For each item, indicate on a five-point scale (1-5 with 5 being high), the extent to which the course meets the criteria as represented by each item.

Course Organization

1. The syllabus adequately outlines the sequence of topics to be covered.

2. The stated course objectives are clear.

3. The outline and sequence of topics is logical.

4. The difficulty level is appropriate for the enrolled students.

5. The course integrates recent developments in the field.

6. Time given to each of the major course topics is appropriate.

7. Course is responsive to the needs of students enrolled in the course.

8. The course is an adequate prerequisite for other courses.

9. The course objectives are congruent with the department curricula.

Readings, Projects, and Laboratory Assignments

1. The reading list (required/recommended) is up to date and represents the work of recognized authorities.

2. Readings are appropriate for level of course.

3. The texts used in the course are well selected.

4. Students are given ample time to complete the assignments/take home exams.

5. The amount of homework and assignments is appropriate.

6. The written assignments and projects are carefully chosen to reflect course goals.

7. A variety of assignments is available to meet individual student needs.

8. Laboratory work is integrated into the course.

9. Students are given the course requirements in writing at the beginning of the course.

10. The assignments are intellectually challenging to the students.

Exams and Grading

1. The exam content is representative of the content and course objectives.

2. The exam items are clear and well written.

3. The exams are graded in a fair manner.

4. The grade distribution is appropriate for level of course and type of students enrolled.

5. The standards used for grading are communicated to the students.

APPENDIX K

Evaluation of Instructor Involvement in Instructional Development and Advising

---

Listed below are several items about instructional development and advising categorized into four areas. For each item, indicate on a five-point scale (1-5 with 5 being high) the extent to which the instructor meets the criteria as represented by each item.

Colleagueship

1. Seeks advice from and discusses with colleagues about effective instruction.

2. Is interested in how colleagues teach.

3. Encourages cooperative teaching arrangements.

4. Is sought by colleagues for advice on instruction.

5. Is knowledgeable about current developments in teaching.

Participation in University Community

1. Is involved in student organized activities.

2. Participates and attends activities in which students are involved.

3. Participates in departmental seminars, activities, projects involving students.

Vocational and Personal Advising

1. Advises students in their future vocational and professional careers.

2. Helps students in their selection of courses.

3. Meets with students informally out of class.

4. Helps students obtain job related experiences that are beneficial to their professional careers.

Academic and Thesis Advising

1. Takes committee membership seriously.

2. Is constructively critical and supportive of students' progress.

3. Provides opportunities for students to conduct publishable research.

4. Is accessible to students.

APPENDIX L

Scoring the Instructor Self-Evaluation Form (ISEF)

The ISEF has four subscales:

1. Adequacy of Classroom Procedures.
2. Enthusiasm for Teaching and Knowledge of Subject Matter.
3. Stimulation of Cognitive and Affective Gains in Students.
4. Relations with Students.

One statement from each of the 11 tetrads is associated with each subscale. Scoring is determined by first reversing the ranks given to each statement within a tetrad (e.g., rank of 1=4) and then adding the reversed numbers across the 11 tetrads. The statements belonging to each subscale by tetrad are as follows:

Set 1	Set 4	Set 7	Set 10
a. 1	a. 2	a. 3	a. 2
b. 4	b. 1	b. 2	b. 1
c. 3	c. 4	c. 4	c. 4
d. 2	d. 3	d. 1	d. 3

Set 2	Set 5	Set 8	Set 11
a. 3	a. 1	a. 2	a. 4
b. 4	b. 2	b. 4	b. 1
c. 1	c. 3	c. 3	c. 2
d. 2	d. 4	d. 1	d. 3

Set 3	Set 6	Set 9	
a. 1	a. 1	a. 1	
b. 3	b. 2	b. 2	
c. 4	c. 4	c. 4	
d. 2	d. 3	d. 3	

For illustration, suppose that the ranks assigned for set 1 were as follows:

Statement	Rank	Score
a	4	1
b	2	3
c	1	4
d	3	2

Statement 'a' belongs to subscale 1 and was given a rank of 4. Reversing the rank yields a score of 1 to be added to the subscale #1 total. Statement 'b' belongs to a subscale 4 is given a rank of 2, etc. Adding across all 11 tetrads yields a maximum score of 44 for a given subscale or a minimum of 11. A score of 44 would mean that each statement in the tetrad was assigned the highest priority by that individual.

Further information about the ISEF may be obtained by contacting Dale C. Brandenburg, Coordinator of Instructor and Course Evaluation System, Measurement and Research Division, 307 Engineering Hall, 1308 W. Green, University of Illinois, Urbana, IL 61801.

Instructor Self-Evaluation Form

Name _____

DIRECTIONS

Following are a number of statements describing some aspects of college teaching. These statements are listed in sets of four. We would like you to examine the items in each set and rank them from *1* to *4* as to the degree to which they apply to you and your course.

In responding, first examine the set and find the item that describes you or your course *MOST,* and assign a rank of *1* to that statement. Then decide which statement describes you or your own course second best, assign a rank of *2* to that item. Do likewise with the two remaining statements, assigning to them ranks of *3* and *4* depending on their degree of applicability to you or your own course.

If you find some items difficult to rank, please show what your choices would be if you have to choose. It is important that you assign a different rank to each item.

Here is an example:

_____1_____ a. I present ideas clearly in class.
_____3_____ b. I enjoy teaching my own course.
_____2_____ c. I stimulate students' interest in the subject.
_____4_____ d. I am fair and impartial in dealing with students.

The person responding to that set indicated that item *a* was most descriptive of him (rank of 1), while item *c* was thought to be the second most descriptive (rank of 2). Items *b* and *d* were given ranks of *3* and *4* respectively, as they applied least to that instructor. You may wish to respond to the questionnaire having in mind one particular course or the totality of the courses that you teach.

SET 1

_____ a. I present thought-provoking ideas.

_____ b. I am sympathetic toward and considerate of students.

_____ c. I assist students in appreciate things they did not appreciate before.

_____ d. I am interested in and concerned with the quality of my teaching.

SET 2

_____ a. My students feel efforts made by them in the course are worthwhile.

_____ b. I am aware of students' needs.

_____ c. I raise challenging questions or problems in class.

_____ d. I make every effort to improve the quality of students' achievement in my course.

SET 3

_____ a. I encourage students to share in class their knowledge, opinions, and experiences.

_____ b. I help students become aware of the implications of the course's subject matter in their life.

_____ c. I remind students to come to me for help whenever it is needed.

_____ d. I analyze previous classroom experience to improve my teaching.

SET 4

_____ a. I take an active, personal interest in improving my instruction.

_____ b. I stimulate and answer questions in class.

_____ c. I relate to students easily.

_____ d. I help students to develop the ability to marshal or identify main points or central issues.

SET 5

_____ a. I organize my course well.

_____ b. I am knowledgeable about related areas aside from my own.

_____ c. I stimulate students' appreciation for the subject.

_____ d. I get along well with students.

SET 6

_____ a. I restate questions or comments to clarify for the entire class.

_____ b. I try to make every course the best every time.

_____ c. I am sensitive to students' feelings.

_____ d. I promote students' satisfaction in learning the subject matter.

SET 7

_____ a. My students gain new viewpoints and appreciations.

_____ b. I have zest and enthusiasm for teaching.

_____ c. I develop a sense of mutual respect with students.

_____ d. I present clear and relevant examples in class.

SET 8

_____ a. I find teaching intellectually stimulating.

_____ b. I make students feel at ease in conversations with me.

_____ c. I stimulate students' interest in the subject.

_____ d. I answer questions as thoroughly and precisely as possible.

SET 9

_____ a. I coordinate different activities of my course well.

_____ b. I look forward to class meetings.

_____ c. I enjoy having students come to me for consultation.

_____ d. My students feel that they can recognize good and poor reasoning or arguments in the field.

SET 10

_____ a. I try to function creatively in teaching my course.

_____ b. I encourage students to participate in class.

_____ c. I actively help students who are having difficulties.

_____ d. I stimulate students' intellectual curiosity.

SET 11

_____ a. I meet with students informally out of class when necessary.

_____ b. I make the objectives of the course clear.

_____ c. I try to make every course the best every time.

_____ d. My students become motivated to study and learn.

APPENDIX M

Name _____

STUDENT EVALUATION

Fixed Response Items*   *Mean*   *s.d.*   *Ranking***

1. Rate the course
2. Rate the instructor
3. Concern for learning
4. Fair grading
5. Course organization
6. Communication skills
7. Stimulation
8. Student learning
9. Workload

*No. of students in course _____

*No. of students completing form _____%_____

**Reference group is _____

Student Comments to Open-Ended Questions

1. Strengths (list 3-4 more common themes) _____
   _____

2. Weaknesses _____
   _____

3. Most beneficial aspects _____
   _____

4. Suggestions _____
   _____

Course _____
      dept.   name   no.

COLLEAGUE EVALUATION

*Classroom Observations**

1. Communication skill _____

2. Ability to question, lead discussion _____

3. Instructor-student interactions _____

4. Model as a scholar _____

*Course Material Appraisals***

1. Content Suitability _____

2. Course Organization _____

3. Evaluation Procedures _____

4. Student Learning _____

*Instructor Involvement in Instruction****

1. Advising _____
2. Participation in Student Groups _____
3. Thesis, Dissertation Advising _____
*Rater(s) _____
**Rater(s) _____
***Rater(s) _____

Semester _____

APPENDIX E (Continued)

DIRECTIONS FOR ICES   SIDE 2

DO NOT WRITE

IN THE

SHADED

AREA

Please use this side of the form for your personal comments on teacher effectiveness and other aspects of the course. Use pencil only in responding to the objective questions on the reverse side.
Objective items 1-3 will be used to compare this course and instructor to others in the department and institution. Data from other items after item 3 would be useful to the instructor for course improvements. Your instructor will not see your completed evaluation until final grades are in for your course.

NOTE:
Someone other than your instructor should collect and mail these forms.

PLEASE WRITE COMMENTS BELOW

A

What are the major strengths and weaknesses of the instructor?

B

What aspects of this course were most beneficial to you?

C

What do you suggest to improve this course?

D

Comment on the grading procedures and exams.

E

Instructor option question

F

Instructor option question

APPENDIX F Sample ICES Instructor Report

FOR: D. Johnson   DEPT ECON   COURSE 302   SECTION C   DEPT CODE 17200   SEMESTER: Spring YEAR 1983

DEMOGRAPHIC DATA IN PERCENTS
NO. OF FORMS COMPLETED: 34

1. PRE-COURSE OPINION TOWARD

	POS	NO OP	NEG	OMIT
INSTRUCTOR	38	62	0	0
COURSE	76	21	0	3

2. COURSE IN:

MAJOR	MINOR	OTHER	OMIT
35	3	62	0

3. SEX:

MALE	FEMALE	OMIT
6	88	6

4. THIS COURSE WAS:

SPECIFICALLY REQUIRED	REQUIRED BUT A CHOICE	ELECTIVE	OMIT
0	71	29	0

5. CLASS STATUS:

FRESH	SOPH	JUNIOR	SENIOR	GRAD	OTHER	OMIT
0	3	44	53	0	0	0

6. EXPECTED GRADE:

A	B	C	D	E	OMIT	*EXP GRADE MEAN=
44	47	6	0	0	3	4.4

GLOBAL CORE ITEM RESULTS

ITEM	WEIGHTS	EXCELLENT 5	- 4	- 3	-- 2	VERY POOR 1	OMIT	SUMMARY STATISTICS MEAN	SD	MDN	CONS	*RELATIVE COMPARISON OF CLASS MEAN GROUP 1: MIXED REQ/FACULTY GROUP 2: ECONOMICS FACULTY
												LOW	AVG	HIGH
1 RATE THE COURSE CONTENT		35 (12)	38 (131(	26 (91(	0 (0)(	0 (0)(	0 (0)(	5.1	0.76	5.1 AVG		1 LOW	AVG	AVG	HI	000X00	000X00
2 RATE THE INSTRUCTOR		47 (16)	38 (131(	9 (3)(	6 (2)(	0 (0)(	0 (0)(	5.3	0.64	5.4 AVG		1	2	00X000	00X000
3 RATE THE COURSE IN GENERAL		26 (9)	47 (161(	18 (61(	6 (2)(	0 (0)(	3 (1)(	5.0	0.83	5.0 AVG		1	2	00X000	00X000

INTERPRETATION GUIDE

THE UPPER PORTION OF THIS PAGE OF THE COMPUTER PRINTOUT CONTAINS PERCENTAGES OF STUDENTS WHO MARKED EACH RESPONSE OPTION FOR THE DEMOGRAPHIC ITEMS. FOR DEMOGRAPHIC #6 THE EXPECTED GRADE MEAN IS CALCULATED USING A WEIGHT OF 5 FOR A, ETC.

GLOBAL ITEM RESULTS: TOP ROWS PRESENT THE PERCENTAGES AND (N) ARE PRESENTED NEXT. LARGER PERCENTAGES AND FREQUENCIES IN ROWS CONTAIN PERCENTAGES; BOTTOM ROWS CONTAIN NUMBERS OF STUDENTS MARKING EACH OPTION. THE SUMMARY STATISTICS ARE CALCULATED USING WEIGHTS INDICATED ABOVE EACH RESPONSE OPTION. FOR GLOBAL ITEMS THE RANGE IS 1-6 WITH 6 MOST FAVORABLE. FOR MOST OTHER ITEMS THE RANGE IS 1-5 WITH 5 MOST FAVORABLE. CONS (CONSENSUS): POSSIBLE VALUES ARE HIGH, AVG OR LOW. HIGH INDICATES CONSIDERABLE STUDENT AGREEMENT.

RELATIVE COMPARISON: CLASS MEAN RATING IS COMPARED WITH ONE OR TWO GROUPS. GROUP 1 IS CAMPUS-WIDE BASED ON REQUIRED/ELECTIVE NATURE OF COURSE AND INSTRUCTOR RANK. GROUP 2 IS DEPARTMENT-WIDE. THE RELATIVE POSITION OF THE CLASS MEAN IS DENOTED UNDER ONE OF THE FOLLOWING FIVE NORM CATEGORIES:

HI--TOP 10%; HIGH AVG--NEXT 20%; AVG--MIDDLE 40%; LOW AVG--NEXT 20%; OR LOW--BOTTOM 10%

THE ROWS CONTAINING AN X AND O'S SHOW THE CLASS AVERAGE RATING IN COMPARISON TO GROUPS 1 AND 2. X INDICATES THE RELATIVE PLACEMENT OF THE MEAN. O'S INDICATE THE RANGE OF UNCERTAINTY. THE RATINGS SHOULD BE READ, FOR EXAMPLE, AS LOW-AVERAGE TO AVERAGE OR HIGH-AVERAGE TO HIGH TO TAKE INTO ACCOUNT THE RANGE OF UNCERTAINTY.

STUDENT RESPONSES TO DEPARTMENTAL CORE ITEMS, INSTRUCTOR SELECTED ITEMS OR COMPLETE FORM ITEMS ARE PRESENTED NEXT. THE RESULTS ARE TO BE INTERPRETED IN THE SAME WAY. HOWEVER, NORMATIVE DATA MAY NOT BE AVAILABLE.

INSTRUCTOR AND COURSE EVALUATION SYSTEM   INSTRUCTOR REPORT D. Johnson   ECON 302 C   17200   NO. FORMS   34   SP 83   PAGE 2

DEPARTMENTAL CORE ITEM RESULTS

RESPONSE LABELS, PERCENTS & FREQUENCIES

									SUMMARY STATISTICS		RELATIVE COMPARISON OF CLASS MEAN

CATALOG ITEM 278
THE INSTRUCTOR WAS CONSCIENTIOUS ABOUT HIS/HER INSTRUCTIONAL RESPONSIBILITIES.
WEIGHTING SCHEME 54321

ECONOMICS FACULTY

	STRONGLY AGREE		--	--	STRONGLY DISAGREE	OMIT	MEAN MDN	SD CONS	LOW! AVG! AVG !AVG!HI
	68 (23)	26 (9)	6 (2)	0 (0)	0 (0)	0 : 0:	4.6 4.6	0.59 AVG	OOXOOO

CATALOG ITEM 101
THE GRADING PROCEDURES FOR THE COURSE WERE:
WEIGHTING SCHEME 54321

	VERY FAIR		--	--	VERY UNFAIR	OMIT	MEAN MDN	SD CONS	!LOW! AVG! ! HI!
	12 (4)	29 (10)	29 (10)	21 (7)	9 (3)	0 : 0:	3.1 3.2	1.14 LOW	LOW! AVG! AVG !AVG!HI

CATALOG ITEM 103
HOW WELL DID EXAMINATION QUESTIONS RE-FLECT CONTENT AND EMPHASIS OF THE COURSE?
WEIGHTING SCHEME 54321

	WELL RELATED		--	--	POORLY RELATED	OMIT	MEAN MDN	SD CONS	!LOW! ! HI!
	15 (5)	41 (14)	29 (10)	9 (3)	6 (2)	0 : 0:	3.5 3.6	1.03 AVG	LOW! AVG! AVG !AVG!HI

CATALOG ITEM 5
WAS THE PROGRESSION OF THE COURSE LOGI-CAL AND COHERENT FROM BEGINNING TO END?
WEIGHTING SCHEME 54321

	YES, ALWAYS		--	--	NO, SELDOM	OMIT	MEAN MDN	SD CONS	!LOW! ! HI!
	38 ( )	50 ( )	( )	( )	3 ( )	0 : 0:	4.2	0.73	OOXOOO

. . .
. . .

INSTRUCTOR SELECTED ITEMS RESULTS

CATALOG ITEM 25
THE INSTRUCTOR CHANGED APPROACHES WHEN THE OCCASION DEMANDED IT.
WEIGHTING SCHEME 54321

	STRONGLY AGREE		--	--	STRONGLY DISAGREE	OMIT	MEAN MDN	SD	MEAN-PROBABLE STRENGTH SD SHOWS AVG AGREEMENT
	70 (19)	26 (7)	4 (1)	0 (0)	0 (0)	0 : 0:	4.7 4.6	0.54	HI RESPONSE WEIGHT 5

CATALOG ITEM 26
I NEEDED MORE DIRECTION.
WEIGHTING SCHEME 12345

	STRONGLY AGREE		--	--	STRONGLY DISAGREE	OMIT	MEAN MDN	SD	MEAN IS IN AVG RANGE SD SHOWS LOW AGREEMENT
	7 (2)	4 (1)	22 (6)	22 (6)	44 (12)	0 : 0:	3.9 4.3	1.21	

CATALOG ITEM 48
THE INSTRUCTOR PROVIDED PRACTICE FOR STUDENTS TO MASTER COURSE MATERIAL.
WEIGHTING SCHEME 54321

	ALMOST ALWAYS		--	--	ALMOST NEVER	OMIT	MEAN MDN	SD	MEAN-PROBABLE STRENGTH SD SHOWS AVG AGREEMENT
	74 (20)	22 (6)	4 (1)	0 (0)	0 (0)	0 : 0:	4.7 4.7	0.52	HI RESPONSE WEIGHT 5

CATALOG ITEM 61
DID YOUR INSTRUCTOR RELATE EXERCISES TO INFORMATION GAINED ELSEWHERE?
WEIGHTING SCHEME 54321

	ALMOST ALWAYS		--	--	ALMOST NEVER	OMIT	MEAN MDN	SD	MEAN IS IN AVG RANGE SD SHOWS AVG AGREEMENT
	52 (14)	33 (9)	11 (3)	0 (0)	0 (0)	4 : 1:	4.4 4.5	0.69	

MESSAGES

. . .
. . .

APPENDIX G

Structured Interview Schedule Outline Used at
Augustana College

Procedure

1. Check to be sure that student understands the nature of "tenure."

2. Explain how the student was selected.

3. Explain how the student's opinion is not to be used as a "vote" for or against promotion.

4. Promise confidentiality.

Questions

1. Strengths and positive comments of the instructor in and out of the classroom.

2. Weaknesses and negative comments of the instructor in and out of the classroom.

3. Instructor demonstration of progress and growth. (For students enrolled in two or more of the instructor's courses.)

4. Rank the instructor with:
   (a) other faculty in the department
   (b) all college faculty

5. Should the instructor receive tenure?

6. Any additional comments.

APPENDIX H

Plan for Peer Evaluation of Teaching Activity
for the Department of Horticulture

INTRODUCTION

Peer evaluation of teaching has been proposed as a desirable input to the administrative evaluation of academic staff members. Results from student questionnaires, while useful in determining attitudes of the instructor, proficiency of presentation and to some degree knowledge of the subject, do not measure adequately such things as choice of subject matter, development of courses and laboratories, and activities outside the classroom such as writing of texts and articles and participation on teaching and courses and curricula committees.

Before peer evaluation can be organized, a definition of the word "peer" is essential. Webster's definition, "one who is on an equal standing with another," could be interpreted to include academic rank and/or technical proficiency and experience in a subject matter area. For this plan, the *technical proficiency* and *experience* will be given high priority.

Student evaluation questionnaires are equally distributed to classes each semester. It does not seem practical to obtain peer evaluation at this frequency. The staff time required would be excessive and many of the items that are appropriate for peer evaluation are not determined by the semester time frame. Consequently, peer evaluation would not be done on a regular scheduled basis but at times when it was needed or requested.

It is essential that the evaluation not be constituted as an adversary relationship between the peers and the instructor. The experience should be both evaluative and helpful and might well be at the request of the instructor whose major purpose would be improvement of the outline for his course.

THE PLAN

Peer evaluations would be made at the direction of the department head

1. for his own use in recommending promotions;

2. at his direction after approval of one of the following requests

a. from the courses and curricula committee,

b. from the instructor being evaluated,

c. at time of adding staff or changing instructors (how should course be changed or dropped).

An evaluation would be scheduled to accomplish one or more of the following:

1. to validate evidence to justify a promotion,

2. to provide assistance to an instructor for developing or improving a course,

3. to assist courses and curricula committees in evaluating course offerings,

4. to provide a systematic method of investigating significant complaints of students about course subject matter.

The Department Head in consultation with the Courses and Curriculum Committee would appoint a committee of three to conduct the evaluation. The committee would normally consist of three professors.

The instructor would assemble the following appropriate items and circulate them to the committee prior to the evaluation:

1. course outlines, daily class schedules, and reference lists (including text);

2. sample problems, examinations, laboratory reports;

3. his own written summary of his significant teaching activities including committee assignments related to teaching, development of laboratories, teaching aids, texts, articles and other teaching innovations;

4. student evaluation summaries of past semesters.

The committee would meet with the instructor and examine and discuss his teaching activities. The members of the committee would not only evaluate the instructor's performance but also make suggestions for improvement. By discussion with the instructor, the committee would rate or validate the items in the written summary of activities. To assure that each member's ideas were included in the report, the report would contain a letter from each of the three. These letters along with the instructor's written summary would then become a part of the instructor's teaching file. This evaluation would not generally include classroom visitation. Depending on the circumstances, the peer evaluation could take on several forms in addition to the basic elements listed above.

APPENDIX I

Videotape Self-Review

Suggestions for Viewing Your Videotape

A. Focus your attention on a *few* lecture skills that are of particular interest to you and that are important to student learning. Select one or more of the following rating guides to concentrate on while you view your videotape.

Rating Guides

Importance and Suitability of Content

Organization of Content

Presentation Style

Clarity of Presentation

Questioning Ability

Establishing and Maintaining Contact with Students

B. If the selected rating guide does not seem relevant to your lecturing style or subject, select another.

C. Space has been provided at the bottom of each rating guide for additional comments which come to mind as you view the tape.

D. Consider the following questions after viewing your videotape.

1. How do your observations and data generated from the Self-Rating Guide compare with your intended goals for the lesson?

2. Are your teaching outcomes consistent with your intent?

SOURCE: Diamond, N., Sharp, G., and Ory, J. C., *Improving Your Lecturing.* Urbana, IL: Office of Instructional Resources, University of Illinois, 1983. Used by permission.

Content: Importance and Suitability

Directions: Respond to each of the statements below by checking the number which best expresses your judgment.

1 = strength
2 = somewhat of a problem
3 = a major problem
4 = not applicable

	1	2	3	4
1. The material presented is generally accepted by colleagues to be worth knowing.	—	—	—	—
2. The material presented is important for this group of students.	—	—	—	—
3. The instructor seemed to match the lecture material to the student's backgrounds.	—	—	—	—
4. The examples used were easily understood by students.	—	—	—	—
5. When appropriate, a distinction was made between factual material and opinions.	—	—	—	—
6. Appropriate authorities were cited to support statements.	—	—	—	—
7. When appropriate, divergent viewpoints were presented.	—	—	—	—
8. A sufficient amount of material was included in the lecture.	—	—	—	—

Other Comments:

Content: Organization

Directions: Respond to each of the state-   1 = strength
ments below by checking the   2 = somewhat of a
number which best expresses   problem
your judgment.   3 = a major problem
                                     4 = not applicable

	1	2	3	4

Introduction

1. Stated the purpose of the lecture. ⎯ ⎯ ⎯ ⎯

2. Presented a brief overview of the lecture content. ⎯ ⎯ ⎯ ⎯

3. Stated a problem to be solved or discussed during the lecture. ⎯ ⎯ ⎯ ⎯

4. Made explicit the relationship between today's and the previous lecture. ⎯ ⎯ ⎯ ⎯

Body of Lecture

5. Arranged and discussed the content so that the organization/structure was made explicit to the students. ⎯ ⎯ ⎯ ⎯

6. Asked questions periodically to determine whether too much or too little information was being presented. ⎯ ⎯ ⎯ ⎯

7. Presented examples, illustrations or graphics to clarify abstract and difficult ideas. ⎯ ⎯ ⎯ ⎯

8. Explicitly stated the relationships among various ideas in the lecture. ⎯ ⎯ ⎯ ⎯

9. Periodically summarized the most important ideas in the lecture. ⎯ ⎯ ⎯ ⎯

Conclusion

10. Solved or otherwise dealt with any problems raised during the lecture. ⎯ ⎯ ⎯ ⎯

11. Restated what students were expected to gain from the lecture material. ⎯ ⎯ ⎯ ⎯

12. Summarized the main ideas in the lecture. ⎯ ⎯ ⎯ ⎯

13. Related the day's lecture to upcoming presentations. ⎯ ⎯ ⎯ ⎯

Other Comments:

Presentation: Style

Directions:	Respond to each of the statements below by checking the number which best expresses your judgment.	1 = strength 2 = somewhat of a problem 3 = a major problem 4 = not applicable

	1	2	3	4

Voice Characteristics

1. Voice could be easily heard. — — — —

2. Voice was raised or lowered for variety and emphasis. — — — —

3. Speech was neither too formal nor too casual. — — — —

4. Speech fillers, ("okay now," "ahm,") were not distracting. — — — —

5. Rate of speech was neither too fast nor too slow. — — — —

Nonverbal Communication

6. Established and maintained eye contact with the class as lecture began. — — — —

7. Listened carefully to student's comments and questions. — — — —

8. Wasn't too stiff and formal in appearance. — — — —

9. Wasn't too casual in appearance. — — — —

10. Facial and body movements were consistent with instructor's intentions. For example, the instructor looked at students while waiting for their responses after asking questions. — — — —

Other Comments:

Presentation: Clarity

Directions: Respond to each of the state-   1 = strength
ments below by checking the   2 = somewhat of a
number which best expresses   problem
your judgment.   3 = a major problem
4 = not applicable

	1	2	3	4
1. Stated the purpose at the beginning of the lecture.	—	—	—	—
2. Defined new terms, concepts and principles.	—	—	—	—
3. Told the students why certain processes, techniques or formulas were used to solve problems.	—	—	—	—
4. Used relevant examples to explain major ideas.	—	—	—	—
5. Used clear and simple examples.	—	—	—	—
6. Explicitly related new ideas to familiar ones.	—	—	—	—
7. Reiterated definitions of new terms to help students become accustomed to them.	—	—	—	—
8. Provided occasional summaries and restatements of important ideas.	—	—	—	—
9. Used alternate explanations when necessary.	—	—	—	—
10. Slowed the word flow when ideas were complex and difficult.	—	—	—	—
11. Did not often digress from the main topic.	—	—	—	—
12. Talked to the class, not to the board or windows.	—	—	—	—
13. The board work appeared organized and legible.	—	—	—	—

Other Comments:

Questioning Skills

Directions: Respond to each of the statements below by checking the number which best expresses your judgment.	1 = strength 2 = somewhat of a problem 3 = a major problem 4 = not applicable

	1	2	3	4
1. Asked questions to see what the students knew about the lecture topic.	—	—	—	—
2. Addressed questions to individual students as well as the group at large.	—	—	—	—
3. Used rhetorical questions to gain students' attention.	—	—	—	—
4. Paused after all questions to allow students time to think of an answer.	—	—	—	—
5. Encouraged students to answer difficult questions by providing cues or rephrasing.	—	—	—	—
6. When necessary, asked students to clarify their questions.	—	—	—	—
7. Asked probing questions if a student's answer was incomplete or superficial.	—	—	—	—
8. Repeated answers when necessary so the entire class could hear.	—	—	—	—
9. Received students' questions politely and when possible enthusiastically.	—	—	—	—
10. Requested that questions which required time-consuming answers of limited interest be discussed before or after class or during office hours.	—	—	—	—

Other Comments:

Establishing and Maintaining Contact With Students

Directions: Respond to each of the state-   1 = strength
ments below by checking the   2 = somewhat of a
number which best expresses   problem
your judgment.   3 = a major problem
   4 = not applicable

	1	2	3	4

Establishing Contact

1. Greeted students with a bit of small talk.
2. Established eye contact with as many students as possible.
3. Set ground rules for student participation and questioning.
4. Used questions to gain student attention.
5. Encouraged student questions.

Maintaining Contact

6. Maintained eye contact with as many students as possible.
7. Used rhetorical questions to re-engage student attention.
8. Asked questions which allowed the instructor to gauge students' progress.
9. Was able to answer students' questions satisfactorily.
10. Noted and responded to signs of puzzlement, boredom, curiosity, etc.
11. Varied the pace of the lecture to keep students alert.
12. Spoke at a rate which allowed students time to take notes.

Other Comments:

APPENDIX J

Evaluation of Course Materials

Listed below are several items about course materials categorized into three major areas. For each item, indicate on a five-point scale (1-5 with 5 being high), the extent to which the course meets the criteria as represented by each item.

Course Organization

1. The syllabus adequately outlines the sequence of topics to be covered.

2. The stated course objectives are clear.

3. The outline and sequence of topics is logical.

4. The difficulty level is appropriate for the enrolled students.

5. The course integrates recent developments in the field.

6. Time given to each of the major course topics is appropriate.

7. Course is responsive to the needs of students enrolled in the course.

8. The course is an adequate prerequisite for other courses.

9. The course objectives are congruent with the department curricula.

Readings, Projects, and Laboratory Assignments

1. The reading list (required/recommended) is up to date and represents the work of recognized authorities.

2. Readings are appropriate for level of course.

3. The texts used in the course are well selected.

4. Students are given ample time to complete the assignments/take home exams.

5. The amount of homework and assignments is appropriate.

6. The written assignments and projects are carefully chosen to reflect course goals.

7. A variety of assignments is available to meet individual student needs.

8. Laboratory work is integrated into the course.

9. Students are given the course requirements in writing at the beginning of the course.

10. The assignments are intellectually challenging to the students.

Exams and Grading

1. The exam content is representative of the content and course objectives.

2. The exam items are clear and well written.

3. The exams are graded in a fair manner.

4. The grade distribution is appropriate for level of course and type of students enrolled.

5. The standards used for grading are communicated to the students.

APPENDIX K

Evaluation of Instructor Involvement in Instructional Development and Advising

---

Listed below are several items about instructional development and advising categorized into four areas. For each item, indicate on a five-point scale (1-5 with 5 being high) the extent to which the instructor meets the criteria as represented by each item.

Colleagueship

1. Seeks advice from and discusses with colleagues about effective instruction.

2. Is interested in how colleagues teach.

3. Encourages cooperative teaching arrangements.

4. Is sought by colleagues for advice on instruction.

5. Is knowledgeable about current developments in teaching.

Participation in University Community

1. Is involved in student organized activities.

2. Participates and attends activities in which students are involved.

3. Participates in departmental seminars, activities, projects involving students.

Vocational and Personal Advising

1. Advises students in their future vocational and professional careers.

2. Helps students in their selection of courses.

3. Meets with students informally out of class.

4. Helps students obtain job related experiences that are beneficial to their professional careers.

Academic and Thesis Advising

1. Takes committee membership seriously.

2. Is constructively critical and supportive of students' progress.

3. Provides opportunities for students to conduct publishable research.

4. Is accessible to students.